1 MONTH OF
FREE
READING

at

www.ForgottenBooks.com

By purchasing this book you are eligible for one month membership to ForgottenBooks.com, giving you unlimited access to our entire collection of over 1,000,000 titles via our web site and mobile apps.

To claim your free month visit:

www.forgottenbooks.com/free1117135

ISBN 978-0-331-39257-9
PIBN 11117135

For support please visit www.forgottenbooks.com

Annual Report

of the officers of the

TOWN OF CONWAY

NEW HAMPSHIRE

For the Fiscal Year Ending

JANUARY THIRTY-FIRST

1939

ANNUAL REPORT

Of the Officers of the

TOWN OF CONWAY

NEW HAMPSHIRE

For the Fiscal Year Ending

JANUARY THIRTY-FIRST

1939

THE REPORTER PRESS, NORTH CONWAY, N. H.

Table of Contents

TOWN OFFICERS

SELECTMEN

Henry J. Hatch,	Term Expires 1939	North Conway
Melvin G. Dennett,	Term Expires 1940	Center Conway
Walter H. Burnell,	Term Expires 1941	Conway

CLERK

Leslie C. Hill   Center Conway

TREASURER

Mellen B. Benson   Conway

COLLECTOR

Ralph L. Grindle   Redstone

ROAD AGENTS

Guy W. Smith, Division No. 1	North Conway
John H. Smith, Division No. 2	Conway
Plummer Potter, Division No. 3	Center Conway

MODERATOR

Arthur H. Furber   North Conway

AUDITORS

Arthur G. Lord	Conway
Robert N. Davis	North Conway

SUPERVISORS

Harry D. Bunker	North Conway
Eugene I. Smith (deceased)	Conway
Perley W. Mudgett	Center Conway

FIRE WARDEN

Edward F. Hurley   Conway

BUDGET COMMITTEE

Clifford H. Craig, Temporary Chairman

John C. Broughton	Arthur A. Greene
William R. Carter	Leslie C. Hill
Neil C. Cates	Frank E. Kennett
Ralph L. Crockett	Herbert C. Lovejoy
Charles O. Dahl	Arthur O. Lucy
Fred W. Dinsmore	Charles E. Poole
Arthur H. Furber	Harry H. Randall
Percy F. Garland	George W. Russell

TOWN WARRANT

State of New Hampshire   Carroll, SS.

To the Inhabitants of the Town of Conway, County of Carroll, qualified to vote in Town Affiairs:

You are hereby notified to meet at the Town House at Center Conway. New Hampshire, March 14, 1939, at nine o'clock in the forenoon to act upon the following subjects:

Article 1.   To choose all necessary Town Officers.

Art. 2.   To see what sum of money the Town will vote to raise and appropriate for the following purposes:

Section A.   Town officers' salaries.

B.   Town officers' expenses.

C.   Election and registration.

D.   Municipal Court.

E.   Town Hall and office expense.

F.   Damage and legal expense.

G.   Police Department.

H.   Fire Department.

I.   Payment on bond issue.

J.   Health Department.

K.   Vital Statistics.

L.   Deficit, 1939.

M.   Town maintenance of highways (summer).

N.   Town maintenance of highways (winter).

O.   Libraries.

P.   Town Poor.

Q.   Old Age Assistance.

R.   Memorial Day.

S.   Soldiers' Aid.

T.   Parks and Playgrounds.

U.   Interest.

V.   State Tax.

W.   County Tax.

Art. 3.   To see what action the Town will take in regard to discounting taxes.

Art. 4.   To see if the Town will vote to authorize

the Selectmen. to distribute the blank inventories. at the time they examine and appraise the property to be taxed.

Art. 5. To see if the Town will vote to authorize the Selectmen to hire upon the credit of the Town, the sum of $60,000 if needed.

Art. 6. To see if the Town will vote to authorize the Selectmen to administer or dispose of any real estate acquired by the Town through Tax Collector's deeds during the present fiscal year.

Art. 7. To see if the Town will vote to authorize the Selectmen to hire upon the credit of the Town a sufficient sum of money to obtain Federal or State Aid on any project agreeable to the Selectmen for which application may be made.

Art. 8. To see if the Town will vote to accept State Aid for the construction of the Class II road known as the River Road, North Conway, N. H., to Bartlett town line, and raise and appropriate. the sum of $1,751.25; or will accept State Aid for the construction of Class V roads and raise and appropriate the sum of $858.95 for said purpose.

Art. 9. To see if the Town will vote to raise and appropriate the sum of $1,000 to resurface about 8/10 of a mile of road in East Conway on the Green Hill Road, known as the Lewis Woods, agreeable to a petition signed by Bert E. Smith and others.

Art. 10. To see if the Town will vote to raise and appropriate the sum of Two Thousand dollars, ($2,000) if necessary, to straighten, resurface and tar the road from the junction of the Gibson and Scribner Cottage road, so-called, to the foot of the Ivy Hill, a distance of one-half mile, agreeable to a petition signed by P. W. Mudgett and others.

Art. 11. To see if the Town will vote to raise and appropriate the sum of $500.00 for weekly band concerts during the months of July and August, 1939, by the Conway Band under the supervision of the Selectmen, agreeable to a petition signed by Herbert L. Yeaton and others.

Art. 12. To see if the Town will vote to raise and appropriate a sufficient sum of money to surface and tar the road leading from the Main street in Kearsarge near the residence of Lester C. Barnes to the top of the hill, past the residence of Norman A. Barnes, said piece of road being approximately 1000 feet long, agreeable to a petition signed by Norman A. Barnes and others.

Art. 13. To see if the Town will vote to raise and appropriate the sum of $75, its proportionate share relative to total valuation of Carroll County to cover deficiency in allotment for maintenance of County Extension Service Recreational Agent to end of fiscal year inclusive of July 31, 1939.

Art. 14. To see if the Town will vote to raise and appropriate the sum of $100.00 to be used for the observance of Memorial Day by the Veterans of Foreign Wars to be used in the Town of Conway, the same sum as was appropriated last year to the Veterans of Foreign Wars for this observance, agreeable to a petition signed by Parker Drown and others.

Art. 15. To see if the Town will vote to raise and appropriate the sum of $150.00 to be used and expended to grade and tarvia Mason Road in North Conway village, from its junction with Pine Street to its junction with Mechanic Street, agreeable to a petition signed by O. Douglass Macomber and others.

Art. 16. To see what sum of money the Town will vote to raise and appropriate or appropriate and hire to put in shape and tar the remainder of Artist Falls Road from Frank Ashnault's residence to the Forest Glen Inn, agreeable to a petition signed by Mrs. Mary A. Thompson and others.

Art. 17. To see what sum of money the Town will vote to raise and appropriate for a Tramp House.

Art. 18. To see if the Town will vote to raise and appropriate a sum not exceeding $750 for the purpose of establishing one or more public dumps, and to appoint a committee to arrange for same if they find suitable locations and report to the next town meeting.

Art. 19. To see if the Town will vote to raise and appropriate $800 to drain Seavey and Kearsarge streets in North Conway.

Art. 20. To see if the Town will raise and appropriate the sum of seven hundred dollars ($700.00) to be used for the promotion and publicity of the Eastern Slope Region, agreeable to a petition signed by Robert N. Davis and others.

Art. 21. To see if the Town will appropriate $301.00, based on 1/100 of 1% of the assessed valuation, for town share of co-operative participation in the White Mountains Region Association.

Art. 22. To see if the Town will vote to raise and appropriate a sufficient sum of money to widen and improve the bridge and its approaches on Main Street, Conway village, agreeable to a petition signed by P. J. Littlefield and others.

Art. 23. To see if the Town will vote to raise and appropriate the sum of Five Hundred ($500) Dollars for the support of Memorial Hospital, North Conway, New Hampshire, agreeable to a petition signed by Ralph L. Crockett and others.

Art. 24. To act upon any other business that may legally come before said meeting.

Given under our hands at said Conway, New Hampshire, this twenty-seventh day of February, 1939.

HENRY J. HATCH
MELVIN G. DENNETT
WALTER H. BURNELL
     Selectmen of Conway

A true copy attest:
HENRY J. HATCH
MELVIN G. DENNETT
WALTER H. BURNELL

BUDGET

OF THE TOWN OF CONWAY

Estimates of Revenue and Expenditures for the Ensuing
Year February 1, 1939 to January 31, 1940 compared
with Actual Revenue and Expenditures of the Previous
Year February 1, 1938 to January 31, 1939

SOURCES OF REVENUE

	Actual Revenue Prev. Year 1938	Estimated Revenue Ens'g Year 1939
From State:		
Interest and dividends tax	$ 3,283 24	$ 3,000 00
Insurance tax	11 66	10 00
Railroad tax	2,481 18	2,000 00
Savings bank tax	2,740 88	2,500 00
For fighting forest fires	39 14	
Forest Reserve	2 65	
Refund on Blister Rust	1 20	
Relief refund	1,198 45	
Bounties	72 00	
From Local Sources Except Taxes:		
Business licenses and permits	300 00	200 00
Fines and forfeits, municipal Court	341 13	300 00
Interest received on taxes and deposits	151 07	300 00
Income of Departments:		
(a) Highway, including rental of equipment	40 00	
(b) Plowing snow	939 80	1,000 00
Town Poor, from County	5 00	
Miscellaneous	2,242 36	
Motor vehicle permit fees	6,115 58	5,500 00
From Local Taxes Other Than Property Taxes:		
(a) Poll Taxes	3,190 00	3,500 00
(b) National bank stock tax	30 75	30 00
Total Revenues from all sources except property taxes	$23,186 09	$18,340 00

PURPOSE OF EXPENDITURES

	Actual Expenditures Prev. Year 1938	Estimated Expenditures Ens'g. Year 1939
Current Maintenance Expenses:		
General Government:		
Town officers' salaries	$ 3,336 25	$ 3,200 00
Town officers' expenses	914 13	900 00
Election and registration expenses	389 87	175 00
Municipal Court expenses	450 13	425 00
Expenses Town Hall and other town buildings	1,450 42	1,000 00
Protection of Persons and Property:		
Police department	1,165 99	1,000 00
Fire department	1,582 93	1,000 00
Moth extermination—Blister rust	200 00	
Health:		
Health department, including hospitals	659 22	150 00
Vital statistics	103 50	125 00
Highways and Bridges:		
Town maintenance, summer	17,301 40	14,500 00
Town maintenance winter	5,464 17	4,000 00
Damage and legal	81 00	200 00
Libraries:		
Libraries	2,100 00	2,100 00
Public Welfare:		
Town poor	7,289 67	7,000 00
Old Age Assistance	1,412 40	1,800 00
Patriotic Purposes:		
Memorial Day and other celebrations	207 24	125 00
Aid to Soldiers and their families	703 81	550 00

Recreation:

Parks and Playgrounds, incl. band concerts	768 00	270 00

Interest:

On Temporary Loans	200 63	300 00
On bonded debt	945 00	855 00

Outlay for New Construction
and Perm. Improve.

Highways and Bridges:

Town construction—W. P. A. Sponsorship	6,382 68	
State Aid Construction—Town's Share	2,009 21	
Timber Salvage Sponsorship	662 70	
Issuing auto permits	333 50	
Sewer Construction—E. Conway drain	494 18	
Publicity	1,000 00	
Refunds	32 33	

Indebtedness:

Payment on Principal of Debt:

Bonds	3,000 00	3,000 00
Deficit of Previous year		7,166 41

Payments to Other Governmental Divisions:

State taxes	6,468 00	8,000 00
County taxes	17,429 75	17,450 00
Payments to precincts	10,366 41	
Payments to school districts	52,603 91	54,638 00
Total expenditures	$147,508 43	$129,929 41

SELECTMEN'S REPORT

To Arthur G. Lord and Robert N. Davis, Auditors for the Town of Conway:

Agreeable with Chapter 43, Article 2, of the Public Statutes of New Hampshire, we submit the following report of our transactions for the Fiscal Year ending January 31, 1939, together with our vouchers.

HENRY J. HATCH
MELVIN G. DENNETT
WALTER H. BURNELL
Selectmen of Conway

INVENTORY

Lands and buildings	$2,790,590 00
Electric Plants	100,500 00
Horses, 94	9,850 00
Oxen, 12	750 00
Cows, 556	26,145 00
Neat Stock, 24	870 00
Sheep, 10	50 00
Hogs, 15	320 00
Fowls, 1860	1,585 00
Fur bearing animals, 65	975 00
Portable mills, 1	750 00
Wood, lbr., etc.	750 00
Gasoline pumps and tanks	10,285 00
Stock in trade	152,375 00
Mills and machinery	63,500 00
Total valuation	$3,159,295 00
Exempted to soldiers	43,670 00
Exempted to blind	1,000 00
Total valuation, exclusive of soldiers' and blind exemptions	$3,114,625 00

2,069 Polls @ $2.00	4,138 00
National Bank stock taxes	30 75
Town Tax rate, per $1,000	31 80
Conway Village Fire District rate	6.70
North Conway Lighting Precinct	3.50
Center Conway Lighting Precinct	3.60

(For amount of assessment, see Tax Collector's Report)

APPROPRIATIONS

Town officers' salaries	$2,700 00
Town officers' expenses	850 00
Election and registration	500 00
Municipal Court	325 00
Town Hall and Office	1,250 00
Police department	900 00
Fire department	1,300 00
Blister rust	200 00
Health department	150 00
Vital Statistics	125 00
State Aid construction, (Eaton Road)	2,000 00
Memorial Hospital	500 00
Soldiers' aid	450 00
Town maintenance—summer	14,250 00
Town maintenance—winter	4,000 00
East Conway drain	350 00
Publicity for winter business	700 00
Publicity, White Mountain Region	300 00
Libraries	2,100 00
Old Age assistance	1,800 00
Town Poor	5,000 00
Memorial Day	225 00
Parks and playgrounds including band concerts	770 00
Damage and legal expense	200 00
Interest	1,445 00
Payment on principal of debt— bond issue	3,000 00

State tax	6,468 00	
County tax	17,429 75	
School tax	48,768 00	

Total town and school appro- priations -	$118,055 75

LESS ESTIMATED REVENUE AND CREDITS

Interest and dividend tax	$3,088 43	
Insurance tax	10 00	
Railroad tax	2,600 00	
Savings Bank tax	2,900 00	
Motor Vehicle permit fees,	4,000 00	
Business licenses and permits	150 00	
Fines and forfeits, municipal court	500 00	
Interest, received on taxes and deposits ·	150 00	
Rentals of highway equipment and town property	850 00	
Surplus	4,681 78	
Total		$ 18,930 21
Amount to be raised for town and school -		$ 99,125 54
Plus overlay		4,088 29
Net amount to be raised by taxation		$103,213 83
Less poll taxes	$4,138 00	
National Bank stock taxes	30 75	
		4,168 75
Amount to be raised by property taxes on which town rate is figured		$99,045 08

COMPARATIVE STATEMENT OF APPROPRIATIONS AND EXPENDITURES FOR THE FISCAL YEAR ENDING JANUARY 31, 1939

	Appro- priation	Expend- iture	Unex- pended	Over- draft
Town officers' salaries	$2,700 00	3,336 25		$ 636 25
Town officers' expenses	850 00	914 13		64 13
Election and registration	500 00	389 87	$ 110 13	
Municipal Court	325 00	450 13		125 13
Town Hall and office expense	1,250 00	1 450 42		200 42
Police	900 00	1,165 99		265 99
Fire department	1,300 00	1,582 93		282 93
Moth Ext.—Blister Rust	200 00	200 00		
Health Department	150 00	159 22		9 22
Vital Statistics	125 00	103 50	21 50	
State Aid—Eaton Road	2,000 00	2,009 21		9 21
Memorial Hospital	500 00	500 00		
Soldiers' Aid	450 00	703 81		253 81
Summer Maintenance	14,250 00	17,301 40		3,051 40
Winter Maintenance	4,000 00	5 464 17		1,464 17
East Conway drain	350 00	494 18		144 18
Publicity—Winter business	700 00	700 00		
Publicity—White Mt. Region	300 00	300 00		
Libraries	2,100 00	2,100 00		
Old Age Assistance	1,800 00	1,412 40	387 60	
Town Poor	5,000 00	7,289 67		2,289 67
Memorial Day	225 00	207 24	17 76	
Parks & Playgrounds incl. Band Conc.	770 00	768 00	2 00	
Damage & Legal	200 00	81 00	119 00	

Interest	1,445 00	1,145 63	299 37	
Payment on bonds	3.000 00	3,000 00		
State tax	6 468 00	6,468 00		
County tax	17,429 75	17,429 75		
Schools	48,768 00	48,768 00		
	$118,055 75	$125,894 90	$957 36	$8,796 51
Net overdraft			7,839 15	
			$8,796 51	$8,796 51

FINANCIAL REPORT

BALANCE SHEET

ASSETS

Cash

In hand of treasurer	$19,540 90	
In hands of officials	1,346 29	
		$ 20,887 19

Accounts Due to the Town:

Due from State:		
Bounties	45 30	
Other bills due Town:		
Snow removal	518 90	
Relief	155 42	
Licenses	626 32	
		1,345 94

Unredeemed Taxes:

Levy of 1937	2,815 49	
Levy of 1936	1,043 82	
Previous years	2,016 87	
		5,876 18

Uncollected Taxes:

Levy of 1938	5,318 89	
Levy of 1937	48 00	

Levy of 1936   5 00
Previous years   5 00

                                                   5,376 89

        Total assets $33,486 20
Excess of liabilities over assets (net debt)   37,166 41

        Grand total $70,652 61
Net debt January 31, 1938 $28,215 46
Net debt January 31, 1939   37,166 41

Increase of debt $ 8,950 95
State purpose for which debt was
    created — Relief and highways

LIABILITIES

Accounts owed by the Town:
Due Town clerk $36 00
Due to school districts:
    (a)   Dog licenses   44 15
    (b)   Balance of appropriation 20,568 00
    (c)   Nat. Forest Reserve
          funds   2 65

                                          $20,650 80
State and Town Joint Highway
    Construction Accounts:
Unexpended balance in State treasury   1 81
    Outstanding Temporary Loans in
    Anticipation of Taxes:
Lincoln D. Young & Co. July
    17, 1939   10,000 00
Lincoln D. Young & Co., Aug.
    15, 1939   10,000 00

                                          20,000 00

Bonds Outstanding:

Refunded long term notes payable $3,000 annually April 1, 1939-1948, inclusive		30,000 00
Total liabilities		$70,652 61
Grand total		$70,652 61

UNIFORM CLASSIFICATION

RECEIPTS

Current Revenue:

From Local Taxes:

Total taxes committed to collector, 1938	$108,791 44		
Less discounts and abatements, 1938	1,060 55		
Less uncollected, 1938	4,572 89		
1 Property taxes, current year, actually collected		$103,158 00	
2 Poll taxes, current year, actually collected		1,790 00	
3 National bank stock taxes		30 75	
Total of current year's collections			$104,978 75
4 Property and poll taxes, previous years, actually collected			6,510 04
5 Tax sales redeemed			5,017 54
Tax sales redeemed (interest)			354 85
From State:			
6 For highways and bridges:			
(d) For State Aid Construction Equip. rental		30 00	
7. Reimbursement for town poor, old age asst., soldiers' aid		1,198 45	

8	Interest and dividend tax	3,283	24
9	Insurance tax	11	66
10	Railroad tax	2,481	18
11	Savings bank tax	2,740	88
12	Blister rust refund	1	20
13	Fighting forests fires	39	14
14	Bounties	72	00

From County:

16	For aid furnished soldiers	5	00

From Local Sources, except taxes:

17	Dog licenses	217	50
18	Business licenses and permits	300	00
19	Fines and forfeits, municipal court	341	13
20	Rent of town property	12	00
21	Interest received on taxes	151	07
23.	Income from miscella-aneous	2 230	36
24	Income from highway equipment	420	90
27	Registration of motor vehicles, 1938 permits	5,981	05
	Registration of motor vehicles 1939 permits	134	53
28	National forest reserve	2	65

	$19,653 94

Total current revenue receipts	$136,515 12

Receipts Other Than Current Revenue:

29	Temporary loans in anticipation of taxes during the year	60,000	00

Total receipts other than current revenue	$60,000 00

Total receipts from all sources $196,515 12
Cash on hand February 1, 1938   26,198 24
                                        _____
    Grand total   . $222,713 36

PAYMENTS

Current Maintenance Expenses:

General Government:

1	Town officers' salaries	$3,336 25
2	Town officers' expenses	914 13
3	Election and registration expenses	389 87
4	Municipal court expenses	450 13
5	Expenses town hall and other town buildings	1,450 42

Protection of Persons and Property:

6	Police department, including care of tramps	1,165 99
7	Fire department, including forest fires	1,582 93
8	Moth extermination— Blister Rust	200 00
9	Bounties	45 30
10	Damage by dogs	173 35

Health:

11	Health department, including hospitals	659 22
12	Vital Statistics	103 50

Highways and Bridges:

14	Truck maintenance	972 78
15	Winter maintenance	5,464 17
16	Town maintenance, summer	14,732 71
18	General expenses of highway department	1,585 91

Libraries:
19   Libraries   2,100 00
     Charities:
20   Old age assistance   1,412 40
21   Town poor   7,289 67
     Patriotic Purposes:
23   Aid to G.A.R. Memorial
        Day exercises   207 24
24   Aid to soldiers and their
        families   703 81
     Recreation:
25   Parks and playgrounds, in-
        cluding band concerts   768 00
     Public Service Enterprises:
26   Issuing auto permits   333 50
27   Publicity   1,000 00
     Unclassified:
     Timber Salvage sponsorship   662 70
29   Damages and legal expenses   81 00
30   Taxes bought by town   5,013 07
31   Discounts and abatements
        ref. and misc.   474 64
                                        _____

     Total current maintenance
        expenses $53,272 69
     Interest;
32   Paid on temporary loans in
        anticipation of taxes   200 63
34   Paid on bonded debt   945 00
                                        _____

     Total interest payments $1,145 63
     Outlay for New Construction
     and Permanent Improvements:
36   Highways and bridges—State
        Aid construction, Eaton
        Road $2,009 21
37   WPA Construction   6,382 68

42 Sewer construction—East Con-
    way Drain   494 18

                                            _____
        Total outlay payments $8,886 07
Indebtedness:
45. Payments on temporary loans
     in anticipation of taxes $ 50,000 00
47   Payments on bonded debt   3,000 00
        Total indebtedness payments $53,000 00
**Payments to Other Governmental
    Divisions:**
51   Taxes paid to State $ 6,468 00
52   Taxes paid to County   17,429 75
53   Payments to precincts   10,366 41
54   Payments to School Dis-
     tricts   52,603 91
     Total payments to Other
        Governmental Divisions $86,868 07
                                            _____
     Total payments for all purposes $203,172 46
Cash on hand January 31, 1939   19,540 90
                                            _____
        Grand Total $222,713 36

SCHEDULE OF TOWN PROPERTY

Town hall, land, buildings, furniture, equip-
    ment $17,000 00
Libraries, land and buildings   25,000 00
Furniture and equipment   5,000 00
Police department, land and buildings,   2,000 00
Highway department, land and buildings;
    Equipment: 2 FWD trucks, 2 snow-
    plows for same; 2 Ross snow plows; 2
    graders; 1 road machine; 1 steamroller;
    3 sanders; hand tools   10,500 00
Parks, commons and playgrounds   5,000 00
Timberlot   1,000 00
                                            _____
    Total value $65,500 00

TAX COLLECTOR'S REPORT

1938

1937 Poll tax items brought forward, total,		$464 13
1937 Poll tax item added		32 00
1938 Resident property taxes	$77,631 01	
1938 Non-resident property taxes	30,817 84	
1938 Bank stock taxes	30 75	
		$108,479 60
1938 Added property taxes		263 14
1938 Poll tax warrant	4,138 00	
1938 Poll taxes added	76 00	
		4,214 00
Total		$113,452 87
1937 Payments to selectmen	$303 06	
1937 Abatements property tax	3 33	
1937 Abatements polls	86 00	
1937 Uncollected polls	48 00	
		$ 440 39
1938 Payments to treasurer	$105,008 75	
Discounts	638 29	
Abatements	422 26	
Advertised—Resident	3,697 33	
Non-Resident	824 21	
Abated Polls	278 00	
Advertised polls	146 00	
Uncollected Pers. Prop. tax	51 35	
Uncollected polls	600 00	
		$111,666 19
		$112,106 58

Balance (paid treas., Feb. 21, 1939) $ 1,346 29

                                        $113,452 87

AUDITORS' CERTIFICATE

Conway, N. H., February 21. 1939

We hereby certify that we have audited the accounts of the Tax Collector of the Town of Conway and find them correct in accordance with the above statement.

A. G. LORD
R. N. DAVIS
                            Auditors.

HIGHWAYS

	Expended	Credits
Appropriation		$14,250 00
Division 1 — Guy Smith, Agent	$4,823 88	
E. Slope Inn, scraping		$ 10 00
E. Slope Inn, drain settlement		100 00
Memorial Hospital, culvert		50 80
		$ 160 80
Division 2 — John H. Smith, Agent	$4,881 50	
L. C. Bolduc, tar		$79 00
		$ 79 00
Division 3 — Plummer Potter, Agent	$5,037 33	
Tar, Frye's Store		$ 10 00
		$ 10 00
General Highway	$1,585 91	
State, N. H., equipment rentals		$ 30 00

Tar, E. Slope Inn,   3 60
State N. H., culvert sold   21 42
F. McCrowe, tar   18 00

                                                   $ 73 02

Truck Maintenance

    . $972 78

    Total credits $ 322 82
Appropriation   14,250 00
Overexpended   2,728 58

                            $17,301 40 $17,301 40

ROAD MAINTENANCE—DIVISION NO. 1

Guy W. Smith, foreman $ 317 43
Guy W. Smith, truck   576 40
George Brooks, truck   12 00
M. N. Eastman, truck   37 20
J. H. Thompson, truck   114 20
Elmer H. Downs, truck   25 20
Myron Hanson, truck   33 60
E. E. Lowd, truck   48 70
Vernon Smith, labor   320 40
Harris Twombly, labor   11 20
George Hanscom, labor   64 80
W. M. King, labor   40 60
Frank Major, labor   8 80
Huntley Allen, labor   5 60
Calvin Colbert, labor   51 40
George Thompson, labor   3 60
George Rancourt, labor   1 00
Dana Greenlaw, labor   17 40
Ernest Ashnault, labor   13 00
Irving Eastman, labor   10 00
Harry Mason, labor   26 60
Chester Cluff, labor   23 40

Donald Mason, labor	2	40
Leon Warren, labor	10	80
Leon Eastman, labor	11	20
Robert Twombly, labor	131	40
John Walker, labor	20	80
Andrew Bergquist, labor	35	20
Horace Northrope, labor	61	80
William Brooks, labor		80
Robert Lucy, labor	3	60
Kenneth Lucy, labor	3	60
Jesse Hale, labor	37	60
John Hopps, labor	24	40
Fred Lucy, labor	33	60
George Fleming, labor	23	20
Fred Rancourt, labor	11	60
E. S. Thompson, labor	13	00
Elmer E. Morrell, labor	8	
Tom Collins, labor	8	
George Armstrong, labor	4	
Walter Davis, labor	4	
Philip Hunt, labor	4	
Clarence Rowe, labor	8	
Clifford Graves, labor	8	
Paul Pond, labor	8	
Earl Grames, labor	8	
A. Varisco, labor	4	
Lawrence Landry, labor	2	
Stewart McLellan, labor	3	
John Munroe, labor	8	
Harold Meader, labor	4	
Harold Tyler, labor	8	
Leon Chick, labor	8	40
Albert Pinette, labor	3	80
George Munroe, labor	8	40
Crosby Hallett, labor	4	80
Walter Munroe, labor	8	40
Ira Snow, labor	8	40

Ernest Peare, labor	16 00
Jerry Cullinane, labor	9 60
George Snow, labor	8 40
Clayton Munroe, labor	6
Fred James, labor	6
Stanley Hunter, labor	8
Raymond Young, labor	8
Thomas Reny, labor	8
Claude Richards, labor	52 80
Peter Fuller, labor	4 80
Ralph James, labor	7 60
Jack Frost, labor	1 20
Harry Mason, labor	8 40
John Ashnault, labor	12
Ray Garland, labor	3
Frank Lougee, labor	3
Fred Bickford, labor	3
Harry Panno, labor	5
Sidney Cluff, labor	5
Jesse Lyman, labor	2
Rockford Brown, labor	3 40
Waldo Lowd, labor	1 80
Walter Scott, labor	1 60
Charles Allard, labor	1
Fred Haley, labor	24
Owen Haley, labor	8
Arthur Seavey, labor	3
Archie Brown, Jr., labor	9
Francis Gallant, labor	7
Elton Eastman, labor	6
W. Galarneau, labor	6
Raymond Twombly, labor	6 60
Carl Tripp, labor	6 80
Dana Haley, labor	9
Homer Bates, labor	7
Wilfred Gallant, labor	7
Jack Spear, labor	6 20

Forest Morrell, labor	4	
S. Graham, labor	4	
L. T. Savard, labor	5	80
Henry Gagnon, labor	3	80
Francis Savard, labor	3	20
Franklin Russell, labor	3	20
Wendell Rancourt, labor	3	20
George Waterhouse, labor	3	20
Everett Waterhouse, labor	5	00
Sam Caddick, labor	3	20
John Walker, labor	3	20
Herbert Willey, labor	3	20
Langdon Walker, labor	3	20
Joe Galarneau, labor		80
Richard Twombly, labor	5	20
Myron Hanson, labor	1	20
E. E. Lowd, gravel	3	55
Harold Sinclair, gravel	5	70
J. Jellison, coal	2	81
Diamond Match Co., coal	18	00
W. J. Maguire, oil	3	42
Otis Johnson, gas, grease	1	95
Conway Supply Co., supplies	4	24
Main Street Garage, supplies	1	15
Carroll Co. Trust Co., gravel	2	80
Kennett Co., coal		85
Eastman Estate, sand	24	90
A. O. Lucy, gravel	3	30
A. W. Chandler, supplies	50	49
B. Eastman, signs	2	75
Central Garage, labor, etc.	1	75
M. N. Eastman, smithing	1	00
N. C. Water Precinct, thawing	26	25
E. T. Savard, labor and material	26	50
Guy Smith, gravel	9	50
Arthur Seavey, stone		30
F. Roland Bean, supplies	8	28

White Mt. F. Sta., supplies	2 44
Whitman Duprey, brick	10 00
E. H. Downs, gas, oil, labor	93 03
Indep. Coal, tarvia	1,790 54
W. Me. For. Nurs., supplies	2 00
W. Mt. Power Co., current	41 25
E. H. Cloutman, smithing	4 05

$4,823 88

ROAD MAINTENANCE, DIVISION NO. 2

John H. Smith, foreman	$209 47
John H. Smith, truck	318 80
Archie Frechette, truck	67 20
Arthur Tibbetts, truck	577 40
Burnham Quint, truck	103 60
W. G. Martin, truck	48 00
William Frechette, truck	95 60
Fred Ritchie, labor	6 40
Lloyd Smith, labor	30 40
Charles Parent, labor	57 00
Frank Greene, labor	14 00
Frank Lackie, labor	12 00
William Meserve, labor	204 40
Frank Oakes, labor	54 00
Ernest Peare, labor	6 40
A. N. French, labor	48 00
Leigh Smith, labor	139 60
C. R. Smith, labor	19 60
William Keith, labor	18 00
Amos Larlee, labor	24 40
A. Gosselin, labor	44 80
H. Porter, Jr., labor	6 40
Thomas Furlong, labor	28 80
Frank Kinslow, labor	6 40
David Turgeon, labor	6 40
Fred Littlefield, labor	47 40
William Hazelton, labor	50 00

M. Baker, labor	25	60
Charles Allard, labor	6	40
Wilfred Frechette, labor	28	80
H. Porter, Sr., labor	6	40
Leon Smith, labor	28	80
Charles Ham, labor	13	20
Harry Mason, labor	28	80
Chester Cluff, labor	28	80
Fred Smith, labor	6	40
DeCosta Smith, labor	50	00
Albert LaFontaine, labor	22	40
Ray Smith, labor	16	00
H. A. Smith, labor	37	20
Obda Smith, labor	6	40
Burnham Quint, labor	9	60
Ed. Burgess, labor	3	20
Homer Gosselin, labor	6	40
Guy Whitaker, labor	9	60
Leavitt Lowd, labor	9	60
Harry Whitaker, labor	3	20
William Murphy, labor	12	80
Harry Mason, labor	14	20
Chester Cluff, labor	14	00
John Lewis, labor	14	80
Warren Chancey, labor	6	80
Oscar Comer, Jr., labor	6	80
Bruce Comer, labor	6	80
Elmer Littlefield, labor	6	80
Maurice Lowd, labor	6	80
Chester Drown, labor	6	80
Abbott Lowd, labor	6	80
Silfred LaFontaine, labor	6	80
Howard Drown, labor	6	80
A. von Baltzer, labor	6	80
John Seguin, labor	6	
Arthur Seguin, labor	6	80
Sidney Welch, labor	3	80

Russell Larlee, labor	11	
Melville Coolidge, labor	11	
Everett Wiggin, labor	1	
S. Hallett, labor	8	
Kenneth Wiggin, labor	8	
Mark Wiggin, labor	8	
Henry Smith, labor	4	
Harold Barbour, labor	1	
Oscar Comer, Sr., labor	1	
Earl Shorey, labor	8	
George Wiggin, labor	1	
Walter Budroe, labor	8	
Fred Thompson, labor	8	
Ben Curran, labor	1	
William White, labor	8	
Luther McDaniel, labor	3	
Arthur Tibbetts, labor	39	
Gordon Stimson, welding		
Arthur Chick, labor	1	
Walter Grant, labor	6	
Alfred Harmon, labor	15	
Avery Allard, labor	1	
Joseph Smith, labor		
Carroll Co. Trust Co., gravel	28	5
Anna Levoy, gravel	6	
John H. Smith, gravel	9	
Conway Supply Co., supplies	20	
Craig's, supplies	10	60
Farrington's, supplies		
Ossipee Oil Co., supplies	6	20
B. & M. R. R., maint. cr.		
signal	62	79
Public Service Co., bridge lights	89	50
H. L. Taylor, labor	5	66
George Richardson, labor	1	00
Indep. Coal Tar, tarvia	1,616	88
R. F. Harmon, labor	5	00

N. E. Haynes, signs   2 00
R. F. Seavey, Town Truck   110 31
E. H. Cloutman, smithing   ·   9 95

                                                            $4,881 50

ROAD MAINTENANCE, DIVISION NO. 3

Plummer Potter, foreman $ 610 67
Plummer Potter, truck   547 20
L. C. Hill, truck   207 60
R. L. Meader, truck   ·   90 60
George Weeks, truck   204 60
P. W. Mudgett, truck   62 40
Leon Shirley, truck   9 60
Mathias Cormier, truck   35 40
Porter Davidson, truck   2 40
M. Dennett, truck   11 60
Calvin Hapgood, labor   3 20
Elmer Morrill, labor   3 20
Seavey's Repair Shop, town trk.   402 28
Fred Fernald, team   14 01
Wilmer Smith, team   20 00
Ward Towle, labor   63 00
Chas. Davidson, labor   20 80
Walter Chick, labor   16 60
Rockford Brown, labor   15 00
Wm. Meader, labor   46 20
Avan Littlefield, labor   22 20
Bert Towle, labor   ـ   60 80
Wm. Jackson, labor   16 60
Chas. Cook, labor.   11 20
Eugene Morrill, labor   2 40
Alden Peterson, labor   :   21 60
Harold Robinson, labor   34 00
Paul Pond, labor   174 40
Roy Garland, labor   46 80
Allen Frye, labor   55 20

Chester Cluff, labor	16 00
Oren Rowe, labor	19 80
Vernal Henderson, labor	9 80
George Grames, labor	42 40
Mathias Cormier, labor	8 20
Wakefield Davidson, labor	17 60
Oliff Mason, labor	22 80
Fred Fernald, labor	4 80
Wilmer Smith, labor	32 80
John McDonald, labor	3 00
Lawrence Miller, labor	11 20
George Snow, labor	35 80
Ernest Peare, labor	59 80
Francis Hatch, labor	27 80
Carl Hatch, labor	12 80
Earl Grames, labor	15 80
Andrew Cook, labor	24 00
Ira Snow, labor	52 40
Leon Chick, labor	5 00
Harold Meader, labor	53 20
Ernest Munroe, labor	18 80
Fred Peare, labor	62 40
Harry Mason, labor	16 20
Almon French, labor	12 00
Ed. Davidson, labor	81 60
Leon Warren, labor	5 20
Sylvester Jackson, labor	15 20
Raymond Graves, labor	4 80
Peter Fuller, labor	7 20
Guy Stiles, labor	5 60
Calvin Stiles, labor	9 40
Clarence Heath, labor	23 40
Norris Hill, labor	3 20
N. H. Granite Co., gravel	3 93
Irving Page, gravel	9 00
Fred Fernald, gravel	1 50
Mat. Cormier, gravel	13 00

Conway Supply Co., supplies	76	
N. E. Haynes, signs	3	
Ed. Davidson, smithing	1	
Ed. Lowd, gravel	1	
Mel. Dennett, supplies	1	
Arthur Brown, supplies	4	
T. Frye, supplies	2	
Ivory Mason, gravel	20	
Emerson Cook, labor	3	
Donald Hill, labor	1	
Elmer Weeks, labor	15	
Everett Bemis, labor	9	
Fred Warren, labor	10	
Harris Twombly, Jr., labor	19	
Archie McDonald, labor	3	
Everett Grames, labor	24	
George Moore, labor	9	
Ralph Wentworth, posts	12	
Glenn Hale, welding	4	
John Shorey, caps	5	
Gerald Stanley, supplies		
Ted Bugbee, labor	3	
Roland Kelley, labor	5	
Irving Stiles, labor	3	
John Yeaton, labor	10	
Clayton Heath, labor	37	
Don. Mason, labor	5	
Anthony Buzzell, labor	3	90
Craig's, supplies	15	80
Burton Garland, labor	6	40
Archie Webster, labor		40
Indep. Coal Tar Co., tarvia	938	31
Elmer Downs, town truck	37	13
Roland Allard, labor	3	20
Leon Wade, Jr., labor	25	60
Clifton Weeks, labor	13	20
John Fuller, labor	7	40

James Kelley, labor 6 00
Eugene Morrill, labor 2 00
Harry Stanley, supplies 3 28
Harold Tyler 20 00
North Con. Water Prec., pumping 51 90
E. H. Cloutman, smithing 8 90

$5,037 33

GENERAL HIGHWAY

R. Grindle, tires, patcher .... $ 10 68
Indep. Coal Tar Co., patchg. tar 1,183 27
Hedge-Matheis, repairs 11 05
W. Burnell, express 54
Files, O'Keefe, blades 91 20
Chamberlain's, repairing mixer 35 85
R. F. Seavey, storage truck 80 00
E. H. Downs, storage truck 60 00
E. H. Downs, repairs road machine 50 16
W. M. For. Nurs., rep. plow 8 75
Brackett-Shaw Co., repairs 27 41
N. Con. Water Prect., trough 20 00
Nellie Potter, trough 7 00

$1,585 91

TRUCK MAINTENANCE
General Bill:

Maine Truck & T. Co., No. C. FWD
   repairs $506 10
Maine Truck & T. Co., Conway FWD
   repairs 11 01
Littlefield Greene Corp., repairs 42
P. F. Garland, ins. on trucks,
   North Conway 17 68
   Conway 17 68
Warren's Express, freight charges 8 20

$ 561 09

Conway Village FWD—R. F. Seavey

Labor	$ 58 80
Supplies and repairs	14 78
Oil	12 00
Grease	1 60
Anti-freeze	3 30
Woodscrew	01
Farrar-Brown Co., battery	29 52
	$ 120 01

North Conway FWD—E. H. Downs

Labor	$ 155 06
Supplies and repairs	37 46
Charging batteries	6 00
Set chains	42 30
Two batteries	18 81
Oil	6 25
Grease	8 00
Armature, etc.	17 80
	$ 291 68

	$ 291 68	$ 291 68
Conway Village total		120 01
General bill		561 09
Total		$ 972 78

EAST CONWAY DRAIN

Appropriation		$350 00
Plummer Potter, foreman	$ 71 43	
Clayton Heath, labor	7 20	
Clarence Heath, labor	39 80	
Ernest Munroe, labor	40 60	
Harold Meader, labor	3 20	
Archie Webster, labor	2 40	
Paul Pond, labor	44 80	
Roland Allard, labor	16 00	
Anthony Buzzell, labor	16 60	

Allen Frye, labor	3 20	
Rockford Brown, labor	9 60	
Stephen Buzzell, labor	11 40	
Joseph Heath, labor	12 80	
James Kelly, labor	9 60	
Ernest Peare, labor	2 00	
Plummer Potter, truck	92 00	
Conway Supply Co., cement and supplies	15 70	
E. F. Hurley, surveying	10 00	
P. W. Seavey, rock	10 00	
J. C. Broughton, frt. and carting	1 85	
Concord Foundry, manhole castings	24 00	
E. L. Webster, lumber	50 00	
Overexpended		144 18
	$494 18	$494 18

STATE AID CONSTRUCTION
Eaton Road

Otis Quint, foreman	$ 387 00
Frank Lackie, labor	290 25
Haven E. Quint, labor	19 20
John McGinty, labor	33 80
Randolph Rowell, labor	127 00
Walter E. Scott, labor	33 80
George M. Fleming, labor	33 80
Harry A. Porter, Sr., labor	62 60
George M. Smith, labor	37 00
Stanley Hunter, labor	16 00
Leslie Lowell, labor	137 00
Rodney Quint, labor	125 60
Elon Harriman, labor	25 60
Clarence Heath, labor	35 20
Clayton Heath, labor	35 20
Chester Cluff, labor	72 80
Alfred Rancourt, labor	22 40
William J. Murphy, labor	28 80

Luther J. McDaniel, labor	28 80
Wilfred J. Frechette, labor	67 20
Walter M. Allard, labor	54 40
Walter I. Allard, labor	32 80
Charles Parent, labor	77 60
George H. Frechette, labor	38 00
Frank T. Lougee, labor	3 20
Benj. Curran, labor	23 20
Burton H. Moore, labor	16 80
Percy R. Drown, labor	36 00
Fred I. Hackett, labor	16 00
Harry H. Whitaker, labor	46 00
Guy H. Whitaker	68 40
Peter Fuller, labor	9 60
Disney G. Welch, labor	80
Jesse Hale, labor	38 40
Belmont D. Whitaker, labor	25 60
Andrew W. Green, labor	9 60
Sidney B. Welch, labor	9 60
Clayton B. Munroe, labor	19 20
Stanley Rogers, labor	16 00
Walter E. Hamilton, labor	19 20
Preston N. Chase, labor	25 60
George W. Keith, labor	6 40
Walter Budroe, labor	16 00
Harry P. Bailey, labor	26 40
Everett M. Wiggin, labor	12 80
Leon A. Shirley, labor	17 60
Herman A. Hutchins, labor	5 40
Phillip P. Watson, labor	17 60
H. Leigh Smith, labor	21 60
Wellington Potter, labor	3 20
Waldo G. Lowd, labor	40 80
Leon B. Hapgood, labor	6 40
Clifford W. Russell, labor	24 00
Kenneth R. Hutchinson, labor	25 20
Edwin S. Newell, labor	9 60

Calvin C. Stiles, labor	
Irving W. Stiles, labor	
Truman Libby, labor	
Charles F. Davidson, labor	1
Archie J. Frechette, labor	
Russell B. Chase, labor	29
Richard A. Watson, labor	3
Carroll Whitaker, labor	5
Bernard A. Smith, labor	6
Maurice H. Lowd, labor	21
Burton W. Lowd, labor	14
Abbott G. Lowd, labor	8
A. J. Gosselin, labor	14
Harry F. Tallman, labor	23
James E. Smith, labor	16 60
Elias Hutchinson, labor	5 80
John Marek, labor	2 00
Gilbert Budroe, labor	14 10
Otis M. Quint, tractor	136 50
Perley W. Mudgett, tractor	153 30
Leo J. Frechette, truck	17 60
Burnham E. Quint, truck	259 80
Wm. G. Martin, truck	93 60
Perley W. Mudgett, truck	267 20
George H. Weeks, truck	50 40
Wm. H. Frechette, truck	72 40
Carroll E. Bryant, truck	127 20
Archie Frechette, truck	27 60
John H. Smith, truck	43 20
Leslie C. Hill, truck	43 20
Leon A. Shirley, truck	17 60
Enos G. Perkins, truck	9 60
Gerald H. Lord, shovel	704 00
Conway Supply Co., materials	122 93
Otis Quint, materials	2 10
Kennett Co., materials	3 78
E. H. Cloutman, smithing	14 80
Dr. Wiggin, first aid	8 00

F. E. Knox, supplies	70
Fred E. Kenison, land	15 00
C. H. Craig Co., supplies	4 43
Randolph Rowell, sand	3 30
Bessie M. Rowell, sand	268 90
Town of Conway, equip. rental	30 00
State Highway Garage, blades	15 62
State Highway Garage, pipe	390 26
State Highway Garage, trucking	62 50
State Highway Garage, paint	8 73
Independent Coal, tar	356 53
Conway Supply Co., posts	52 50

Total			$6,027 63
	State	Town	Total
Apportionment	$4,022 04	$2,011 02	$6,033 06
Expenditures	4,018 42	2,009 21	6,027 63

SPONSORS CONTRIBUTION, W. P. A. PROJECTS

Authorized	$5,000 00

MILL STREET PROJECT

John H. Smith, foreman	$248 76
John H. Smith, truck	348 13
Burnham Quint and truck	514 30
Archie Frechette and truck	360 00
M. G. Martin and truck	252 00
William Frechette and truck	68 40
Lloyd Smith, labor	8 00
Leigh Smith, labor	20 40
Ernest Peare, labor	13 07
H. C. Lovejoy, gravel	282 70
Conway Supply Co., supplies	49 37
N. E. Met. Culv. Co., culvert	113 86
C. Co. Trust Co., gravel	97 50

E. H. Cloutman, smithing	37 20
F. W. Bean, supplies	8 11
A. W. Chandler, supplies	17 40

Total Spon. Contribution	$2,439 20

CLUFF CUTOFF ROAD PROJECT

Plummer Potter, foreman	$153 56
Perley W. Mudgett, foreman	138 09
Harry Mason, labor	3 50
R. Graves, labor	8 23
Harold Graves, labor	2 34
Chester Graves, labor	3 33
A. N. French, team	52 50
R. L. Meader, truck	111 80
E. L. Webster, team	116 39
Porter Davidson, truck	28 20
Walter Chick, team	24 38
Ivory Mason, team	17 50
S. C. Buzzell, team	123 38
R. E. Ballard, team	49 00
R. F. Webster, team	39 39
James Davidson, team	32 39
P. W. Mudgett, truck	281 40
P. W. Mudgett, tractor	93 00
Dean Webster, team	7 00
L. C. Hill, truck	131 00
Otis Quint, truck	120 00
George Weeks, truck	81 00
W. G. Martin, truck	19 20
Conway Supply Co., supplies	40 67
M. G. Dennett, tools and supplies	45 95
R. F. Seavey, supplies	1 00
Roy Garland, supplies	45
P. W. Mudgett, supplies	13 40
C. E. Buzzell, culvert	213 75
C. A. Hill, culvert	40 00
Hedge, Matheis Co., cable	36 63

H. S. Mason, post and gravel	84 95
W. R. Burnell, supplies	12 00
Warren's Express, freight	3 05

Total, Sponsors Contribution $2,128 43

SWETT STREET IMPROVEMENT PROJECT

Guy W. Smith, foreman	$ 96 75
Guy W. Smith, truck	44 40
E. E. Lowd, truck	95 40
George Brooks, truck	104 80
Myron Davis, truck	8 40
Fred Lucy, labor	2 00
Vernon Smith, labor	22 00
Harold Sinclair, sand	21 00
E. E. Lowd, gravel	57 90
Conway Supply Co., supplies	22 56
F. W. Bean, supplies	38 76
Main Street Garage, supplies	2 00
Elmer H. Downs, supplies, town truck	3 90

Total Sponsors Contribution $ 519 87

DIANA'S BATHS ROAD PROJECT

Guy W. Smith, foreman	$139 50
Guy W. Smith, truck	190.40
George Brooks, truck	66 00
Myron Davis, truck	88 80
M. N. Eastman, truck	74 40
A. O. Lucy, tractor	4 00
Fred Lucy, team	195 13
Guy W. Smith, team	108 50
Vernon Smith, labor	95 20
Claude Richards, labor	2 80
George Cox, labor	4 40
F. W. Bean, supplies	7 20
Guy Smith, gravel	87 40

Arthur Lucy, gravel	33 00	
Conway Supply Co., supplies	107 40	
M. N. Eastman, smithing	6 90	
Irving Eastman, smithing	7 40	
N. E. Met. Culv. Co., culvert	51 00	
J. H. Thompson, scraper	15 00	
W. H. Burnell, freight	50	
E. H. Cloutman, smithing	10 25	
Total Sponsors Contribution		$1,295 18

Total costs, Sponsors Contribution, $6,382 68

Winter Maintenance

General Bill

Maine Steel, Inc., reprs. Con. plow	$149 85	
Maine Steel, Inc., reprs. No. Con.		
plow	50 16	
Eastern Trac. & Eq. Co., oil	4 50	
Ray Rd. Equip., 2 Galion sanders	375 25	
Ray Rd. Equip., repairs	6 56	
A. W. Chandler, supplies	1 80	
Harold Goodwin, repairs	1 75	
Gordon Stimson, welding Con. plow	14 50	
R. F. Seavey, repairs Con. plow	67 49	
E. H. Downs, repairs No. Con. plow	68 85	
John Broughton, freight	55	
A. G. Nelson, plowing	92 00	
Town of Eaton, plowing	14 00	
G. S. Moore, plowing	15 00	
Conway Supply Co., plowing	1 50	

$ 863 76

Winter Maint. Contd., No. Conway FWD, E. H. Downs

Gasoline	$ 104 88
Oil	11 65

Storage	50 00	
Harold Eastman, driver	50 77	
Lorenzo Savard, driver	60 76	
Geo. Thompson, helper	32 60	
John Doty, helper	1 50	
Ellsworth Nash, helper	13 25	
Francis Ashnault, helper	21 50	
S. Buswell, helper	5 75	
		$ 352 66

Winter Maint., Contd., Conway FW.D, R. F. Seavey

Gasoline	$ 147 77	
Oil	8 55	
Storage	40 00	
R. F. Seavey, driver	120 26	
Roy Clemons, driver	90 40	
Plummer Potter, helper	6 00	
Leon Howard, helper	74 75	
Roger Seavey, helper	5 00	
Elmer Littlefield, helper	46 75	
		$ 539 48

Winter Maint., Contd., Ross Plows
General Bill

Files & O'Keefe, blades	$ 52 80	
Burch Corp'n, repr. parts, and reprs.	25 70	
Clarke-Wilcox Co., parts and reprs.	172 72	
Me. Trk. & Tract. Co., repairs	36 90	
Gordon Stimson, welding	1 50	
		$ 289 62

Winter Maintenance, Contd.—Ross Plows

Walter Mason, plowing	$ 256 27	
Walter Mason, put away plow	3 00	
Harley Mason, repairs	6 05	
Donald Mason	2 13	

Ivory Mason, plow to shop and ret.   16 60
                                    ————————
                                                    $ 284 05

T. H. Thompson, plowing $ 432 94
Central Garage, care and reprs.   70 05
S. E. Caddick, plow and plowing   102 50
                                    ————————
                                                    $ 605 49

Winter Maintenance Cont'd—Sanding

Plummer Potter, truck $243 20
George Weeks, truck   18 60
Smith Allard, truck   8 40
Harlan Ballard, truck   19 20
L. C. Hill, truck   19 20
Elmer Downs, truck   1 20
Ed. Munroe, truck   18 50
Guy W. Smith, truck   360 73
Perley W. Mudgett, truck   3 00
Randall Meader, truck   25 00
Walter Mason, truck   29 90
Leon Shirley, truck   9 00
Arnold Hill, truck   18 00
Arthur Tibbetts, truck   120 40
John Smith, truck   137 80
Harry D. Bunker, repairs   2 95
Conway Supply Co., dynamite   3 35
A. O. Lucy, sand   16 95
John H. Smith, sand   40 65
Harold Sinclair, sand   30 30
Minnie Davis, sand   1 65
Diamond Match Co., supplies   3 00
Johnson's Ser. Sta., repairs   1 04
Guy Smith, sand   45
Roland Bean, supplies   1 25
Kennett Co., supplies   85
Main Street Garage, supplies   45

Guy W. Smith, foreman	214 14
Vernon Smith, labor	186 13
Ben Harding, labor	2 33
Frank Tripp, labor	10 83
Byron Bemis, labor	2 33
Ted Quint, labor	1 33
Harris Twombly, labor	11 20
Arnold Caddick, labor	6 67
Ernest Ashnault, labor	1 60
Calvin Colbert, labor	7 67
John Tripp, labor	8 67
Tom Reny, labor	9 77
Frank Major, labor	6 00
Harold Eastman, labor	1 00
Ethan Hersey, labor	2 50
Roger Bertwell, labor	1 00
Richard Twombly, labor	22 13
Jerry Cullinane, labor	2 33
Frank James, labor	4 67
Myron Hanson, labor	18 40
Donald Wakefield, labor	3 20
Walter Scott, labor	6 40
John H. Smith, foreman	86 97
Fred Ritchie, labor	23 73
Charles Parent, labor	5 60
Edward Chesley, labor	75 09
William Meserve, labor	31 40
A. D. Tibbetts, labor	2 80
John Lewis, labor	10 27
Leigh Smith, labor	66 20
Harry Mason, foreman	16 00
Ernest Peare, labor	6 20
George Snow, labor	3 00
Walter Chick, labor	6 83
Clifton Weeks, labor	5 67
Leon Warren, labor	1 50
Preston Mason, labor	5 17

Roy Garland, labor	5
Allen Frye, labor	2
Donald Mason, labor	5
Ira Snow, labor	21
Leslie Lowell, labor	1
Leon Chick, labor	4
Paul Pond, labor	42
Fred Peare, labor	25
Lawrence Miller, labor	7
Sylvester Jackson, labor	85
Ward Towle, labor	3
Harold Baker, labor	2
George Weeks, labor	6
Bert Hewey, labor	1
Clifford Graves, labor	10
Richard Bransfield, labor	19
Reginald Fuller, labor	1
Clarence Heath, labor	4
Fred Woodman, labor	50
Lawrence Whiteman, labor	1
Fred Lucy, labor	2
Wilmer Smith, labor	6 00
James Kelly, labor	
Plummer Potter, foreman	1
Rockford Brown, labor	
Clifton Weeks, labor	6
Harvey Mason, labor	1 40
Harold Tyler, labor	1 33
George Johnson, labor	3 20
Nathaniel Hill, labor	10 00
George Hill, labor	9 60
Archie Brown, labor	3 60
Leon Eastman, labor	1 20

Total	$ 2,529 11
Appropriation, Winter Maintenance	$4,000 00
Sanding	$2,529 11

General Bill	863 76	
No. Conway FWD Plow	352 66	
Conway FWD Plow	539 48	
Ross Plows and plowing	1,179 16	
Overdrawn		1,464 17
	$5,464 17	$5,464 17

SUMMARY OF WINTER MAINTENANCE

Received from plowing snow from Albany, Bartlett, Madison	$420 90	
Due for plowing snow	518 90	
Total		$ 939 80
Net cost of winter maintenance		$4,524 37

TOWN OFFICERS' SALARIES

Appropriation		$2,700 00
Henry J. Hatch	$700 00	
Melvin G. Dennett	697 50	
Walter H. Burnell	841 25	
John C. Broughton	118 50	
Ralph L. Grindle	600 00	
Robert N. Davis	32 00	
Arthur G. Lord	32 00	
Mellen B. Benson	135 00	
Arthur H. Furber	30 00	
Leslie C. Hill	150 00	
Overdrawn		636 25
	$3,336 25	$3,336 25

TOWN OFFICERS' EXPENSES

Appropriation		$ 850 00
Henry J. Hatch	$ 322 45	
Melvin G. Dennett	175 26	
Walter H. Burnell	217 04	

John C. Broughton	21 28	
Ralph L. Grindle	28 10	
A. D. Davis & Son, bond treas.	25 00	
Conway Ins. Agcy, bond clerk	25 00	
John N. Leighton, bond collector	100 00	
Overdrawn		64 13
	$ 914 13	$ 914 13

ELECTION AND REGISTRATION

Appropriation		$500 00
Supervisors		
Harry D. Bunker	$136 03	
Perley W. Mudgett	66 00	
Eugene I. Smith	55 84	
Ballot Clerks		
W. R. Carter	16 00	
Neil C. Cates	22 00	
Robert H. Kennett	8 00	
Eldred M. Littlefield	16 00	
Arthur G. Lord	8 00	
Herbert C. Lovejoy	6 00	
Maurice M. Lovejoy	16 00	
Fred H. Sawyer	22 00	
The Reporter Press, ballots	18 00	
Total	$389 87	
Unexpended	110 13	
	$ 500 00	$ 500 00

MUNICIPAL COURT

Appropriation		$ 325 00
E. I. Smith, Justice salary	$250 00	
C. E. Poole, Justice salary	50 00	
C. E. Poole, associate justice	141 00	
Reporter Press, stationery	9 13	
Overdrawn		125 13
	$ 450 13	$ 450 13

TOWN HALL AND OFFICE EXPENSE

Appropriation		$1,250 00
Pauline Dennett, typing	$49 25	
Edson C. Eastman Co., supplies	48 08	
Pub. Svce. Co. N. H., current	24 00	
Reporter Press, reports and supplies	485 42	
Henry J. Hatch, telephone	22 07	
John C. Broughton, telephone	8 03	
Melvin G. Dennett, telephone	35 49	
Walter H. Burnell, telephone	27 55	
N. H. Assessors Ass'n., dues	2 00	
Conway Print Shop, supplies	20 00	
Guy C. Mason, Jan. and labor	77 50	
R. L. Grindle, postage	75 00	
Emma F. Garland, budget dinner	15 00	
Lloyd Garland, gov't. env.	37 48	
C. H. Carter, regr. transfers	55 89	
P. F. Garland, ins. pub. bldgs.	142 50	
Wheeler & Clark, stationery	1 03	
John Leighton, fire extinguisher	26 00	
State Board Welfare, stationery	60	
Ed. Little Co., supplies	5 11	
Conway Supply Co., roofing	125 75	
Oliff Mason, labor	13 50	
Ira Snow, labor	1 50	
A. W. Chandler, supplies	65 42	
Robert Johnson, labor	10 00	
E. A. Pitman, wiring	15 25	
L. C. Hill, clerk's office ex.	60 00	
L. S. & Harmon, stationery	1 00	
Overexpended		200 42
	$1,450 42	$1,450 42

POLICE DEPARTMENT

Appropriation		$900 00
L. T. Savard, police duty	$10 15	
E. R. Stern, police duty	10 75	

H. L. Taylor, police duty	289 59
Lorenzo A. Savard, police duty	418 73
Frank Greene, police duty	19 25
David Hagar, police duty	3 50
Frank Knox, police duty	4 00
Otis Quint, police duty	10 50
Arnold Caddick, police duty	3 80
A. M. Miller, police duty	6 50
Robert Bly, police duty	2 00
Alton Eastman, police duty	2 40
F. Bickford, police duty	2 00
Geo. Gaudette, Jr., police duty	2 00
Frank Allard, police duty	15 50
Jesse Lyman, police duty	20 20
George Robinson, labor	5 80
John Ashnault, labor	16 20
Amos Ashnault, labor	3 00
White Mt. Power Co., light	16 10
A. D. Davis & Son, insurance	18 75
Conway Supply Co., wood	42 00
Roland Thompson, painting jail	56 50
J. N. Leighton, care tramps	86 42
E. R. Stern, care tramps	10 75
Ernest Richardson, P.M., C.O.D. uniform	20 13
Carter's Dept. Store, uniform	36 25
Ward & Poole, supplies	6 46
F. R. Bean, supplies	3 95
A. W. Chandler, supplies	17 87
Harry Patten, bal. uniform	3 50
White Mt. Laundry, laundry	1 44

Overdrawn   265 99

Total $1,165 99 $1,165 99

FIRE DEPARTMENT

Appropriation $1,300 00
E. F. Hurley, forest fires   93 85

State Forester, fire pumps	22 50	
Fryeburg Fire Department	15 50	
L. T. Savard, forest fires	21 78	
No. Conway Fire Dept.	265 50	
Conway Village Fire Dist.	1,163 80	
Overdrawn		282 93
Totals	$1,582 93	$1,582 93

BOUNTIES

John C. Broughton	$ 60	
Henry J. Hatch	8 70	
M. G. Dennett	20 20	
W. H. Burnell	15 60	
Total		$ 45 .10

DAMAGE BY DOGS

Received by L. C. Hill, Clerk and paid to Treasurer		$217 50
Paid Thos. Hunter, settlement	$ 2 00	
Brown & Saltmarsh, tags and blanks	16 15	
G. E. Densmore, damages	102 00	
Philip Davis, Sr., damages	35 00	
L. C. Hill, 91 licenses	18 20	
Total	$173 35	
Balance due school district	44 15	
	$217 50	$217 50

HEALTH DEPARTMENT

Appropriation		$150 00
Paid Drs. Shedd	$159 22	
Overdrawn		9 22
Total	$159 22	$159 22

VITAL STATISTICS

Appropriation		$125 00
Paid		
Preston Smart, reporting	$ 1 50	
Drs. Shedd, reporting	7 50	
Dr. Wiggin, reporting	12 25	
Dr. Smith, reporting	9 00	
Leslie C. Hill, reporting	73 25	
	$ 103 50	
Unexpended	21 50	
	$ 125 00	$ 125 00

LIBRARIES

Appropriation		$2,100 00
Paid Ruth G. Kennett, treas.	$2,100 00	
	$2,100 00	$2,100 00

MEMORIAL DAY

Appropriation		$225 00
Paid Chas. E. Hayes, care of		
Veterans' graves	$ 7 24	
Ralph W. Shirley Post	100 00	
Saco Valley Post	100 00	
	$207 24	
Unexpended	17 76	
	$225 00	$225 00

ACCOUNTS OF THE MEMORIAL DAY PROGRAMS AS EXPENDED BY THE PATRIOTIC SOCIETIES

Ralph W. Shirley Post, No. 46, Inc., The American Legion

Boston Regalia Co., flags,	$15 65
M. D. Jones Co., grave markers	9 66

Ernest L. Mills, speaker and
    travel   17 00
Conway Brass Band, music   50 00
John B. Varick Co., ammunition   4 17
French's Radio Service, loud
    speaker   1 50
Wreaths, 144 @ .20   28 80

                                      $126 78

Saco Valley Post, No. 385, Veterans of Foreign Wars

Dinner $23 38
Dishwashing labor   4 00
Telephone calls   5 70
Joliette SS Club Drum Corps   45 00
Flags for graves   5 76
Firing Squad nine men   8 67
Wreaths for graves   15 50
Ribbons and letters   2 00
Two guest speakers: one, North
    Conway; one, Conway   5 00

                                        $115 01

BLISTER RUST

Appropriation $200 00
Paid John H. Foster, State
    Forester $200 00

                        $200 00 $200 00

Financial Statement, 1938, Town of Conway
TOWN PROGRAM

Crew cost $198 80
Foreman cost   50 00

Total expended $248 80
Received from town   200 00

Expended from town's funds	198 80	

Balance due town		1 20
Area covered	642 acres	
Currant and gooseberry bushes		
destroyed	7,977	
Local men employed	7	

OLD AGE ASSISTANCE

Appropriated		$1,800 00
Paid Carroll Co. Treas.	$ 643 40	
Paid Dept. Pub. Welfare	769 00	
	$1,412 40	
Unexpended	387 60	
Total	$1,800 00	$1,800 00

TOWN POOR

Appropriation		$5,000 00
John C. Abbott, milk	$ 119 07	
Dr. Boothby, care	70 50	
Carroll County Home, care	937 37	
A. W. Chandler, fuel	37 75	
Theresa Frye, food	52 00	
H. Guerette, board	96 26	
Dr. Holt, glasses	5 00	
F. P. Howard, rent	50 00	
Hastings & Son, wood	32 00	
Kennett Co., fuel	13 50	
H. D. Bunker, rent	110 00	
F. E. Littlefield, rent	20 00	
Meader-Sabin, food	100 00	
P. Mudgett, wood	8 00	
Memorial Hospital, care	594 63	
Public Service Co., lights	25 28	
J. Richardson, milk	14 53	
H. J. Hatch, milk	52 30	

L. T. Savard, food	84	84
Shell Oil Co., fuel	13	50
E. F. Swett, rent	76	50
F. S. Allard Co:, food	98	78
Treas. U.S.A. — Sew. Project contr.	689	00
W. H. Burnell, sew. proj. rent	185	00
J. C. Broughton, freight	2	00
J. W. Kenison, food	96	56
M. G. Dennett, food	38	73
Farrington's, food	705	68
Craig's, clothing and food	108	29
Conway Supply Co., fuel	29	50
Edgewood, milk	58	20
E. L. Webster, milk	22	11
Willey Farm, milk	110	28
James O. Flint, food	85	00
Irene Boothby, rent	16	00
A. I. Hodgdon, care	430	38
Koplow Trim. Co., supplies	70	97
Dr. Wiggin, care	141	20
Roberts Market, food	227	00
Dr. Mazzoli, care	88	50
Drs. Shedd, care	86	00
Central Garage, trans.	7	00
J. W. Robertson, rent	20	50
J. P. Carter, glasses	17	50
A. H. Furber, rent	41	75
A. L. Potter, fert.	6	60
J. Prescott, board	212	76
C. Robinson Co., paper	6	17
Dr. Smith, care	36	60
D. Smith, board	26	33
F. Roland Bean, food	43	00
H. M. Curran, rent	12	50
Osteop. Hospital, care	158	66
O. B. Merrill, rent	20	00

Harry Thompson, rent	10 00
Littlefield Garage, rent	20 00
K. McGee, rent	12 00
Marg. Weeden, care	14 00
C. R. Head, transportation	5 00
Dr. Remick, clo.	28 15
A. M. Miller, fuel	1 00
Dr. Winslow, care	30 00
Dr. Bray, care	64 50
Coos County Hospital, care	31 00
I. Baker, repr. S. Mach.	2 00
Fryeburg Dairy, milk	5 04
Newell Smith, food	50 00
Webster Store, clothing	25 74
Ed. Warren, fuel	7 00
A. Zimmerman, rent	40 00
R. Wentworth, care	35 00
Diamond Match Co., fuel	30 80
A. A. Greene, rent	15 00
L. Thompson, care	3 00
Cancer Commission, care	72 00
Mod. Market, Roch., food	9 00
J. Annis, plow garden	4 00
J. McFayden, rent	63 00
Cash allowances	300 81

$7,289 67

Reimbursement received	$1,272 63	
Reimbursement due town	28 00	
		$1,300 63
Overdrawn		989 04
	$7,289 67	$7,289 67

SOLDIERS' AID

Appropriation		$450 00
Savard's Market food	$161 94	
Shell Oil Co., fuel	26 82	
F. Roland Bean, food	6 00	
Ambrose Stuart, milk	69 99	
Carter's Dept. Store, clothing	3 23	
G. B. Wyman, milk	32 40	
M. G. Dennett, food	36 60	
Craig's, clothing and food	102 91	
Carroll County Trust Co., rent	10 60	
Kennett Co., fuel	33 50	
Willey Farm, milk	77 80	
Dr. Wiggin, care	42 70	
Memorial Hospital, care	79 82	
Dr. Mazzoli, care	14 50	
Theresa Frye, food	5 00	
	$703 81	
Reimbursed by Limerick, Me.		250 76
Due from Limerick, Me.		24 00
Unexpended	20 95	
Total	$ 724 76	$ 724 76

PARKS AND PLAYGROUNDS

Appropriaton		$270 00
Paid		
G. Rancourt, Redstone	$50 00	
Mrs. Minerva Sawyer, Conway	75 00	
R. G. Warren, No. Conway	125 00	
Walter Chick, lab. Ctr. Conway	3 00	
Robert Johnson, care Ctr. Conway	15 00	
	$268 00	
Unexpended	2 00	
	$270 00	$270 00

DAMAGE AND LEGAL EXPENSES

Appropriation		$200 00
Arthur A. Greene, services in 1937 and 1938	$ 75 00	
Edward F. Hurley, survey and map	3 00	
Conway Photo Shop, photography	3 00	
	$ 81 00	
Unexpended	119 00	
	$200 00	$200 00

TAXES BOUGHT BY TOWN

Paid R. L. Grindle, Collector for 1937	$5,013 07

INTEREST

Appropriation		$1,445 00
Paid Carroll Co. Trust Co.	$ 945 00	
Lincoln R. Young & Co.	200 63	
	$1,145 63	
Coupons not presented	299 37	
	$1,445 00	$1,445 00

BAND CONCERTS

Appropriation		$500 00
Paid Dana J. Farrington, leader	$500 00	
	$500 00	$500 00

MEMORIAL HOSPITAL

Appropriation		$500 00
Paid Memorial Hospital	$500 00	
	$500 00	$500 00

AUTO PERMIT EXPENSE

Paid Leslie C. Hill, 1334 permits	$333 50

TEMPORARY LOANS

Paid Hartford Conn. Trust Co.		$10,000 00
Lincoln R. Young Co.		40,000 00
		$50,000 00

PAYMENT ON BOND ISSUE

Appropriation		$3,000 00
Paid Bonds 1, 2, 3, Due April 1, 1938, through the Carroll County Trust Co.	$3,000 00	
	$3,000 00	$3,000 00

SCHOOLS

Balance due schools, Jan. 31, 1938	$23,825 00	
School warrant for year 1938,.	48,768 00	
Income from dog taxes, 1937	578 91	
Paid on warrant		$52,603 91
Balance due schools, Jan. 31, 1939		20,568 00
	$73,171 91	$73,171 91

STATE OF NEW HAMPSHIRE

State Tax warrant for 1938		$6,468 00
Paid State Treasurer	$6,468 00	
	$6,468 00	$6,468 00

CARROLL COUNTY

County Tax warrant for 1938		$17,429 75
Paid County Treasurer	$17,429 75	
	$17,429 75	$17,429 75

PUBLICITY

Appropriations		$1,000 00
Paid Charles O. Dahl, treas.	$300 00	
Noel Wellman, treas.	700 00	
Total	$1,000 00	$1,000 00

REFUNDS

Paid Earl Harriman proceeds from auction
sale of portable mill to Ernest Nelson
after deduction 1937 tax sale, $23 58

PERAMBULATING THE TOWN LINES

Edward F. Hurley and helper $ 39 80
Reimbursement by Bartlett   17 50

                                          _____

                                          $ 22 30

REDEMPTION BACK TAXES SOLD
INDIVIDUALS

Paid Mrs. Anna Lovejoy as received
from H. O. L. C. $280 57

CLEARANCE, 1937 TAX

Paid R. L. Grindle, collector tax
received from Home Owners Loan
Corporation $121 94
Paid R. L. Grindle, collector, bank tax for
First Nat. Bank of Rochester received
direct   8 75

                                          _____

                                          $130 69

TIMBER SALVAGE LANDING

Harry C. Batchelder, lot rental	$ 29 17
R. F. Harmon, boom expense	10 10
B. & B. Trans. Co., frt. on chains	2 95
Brown Co., trustees, chains	37 50
F. Rawson, towing boom	2 63
Conway Supply Co., scalers house	195 93
Craig's, hardware for same	3 72
Conway Insurance Agcy. fire ins.	3 00
W. C. Marston, stove	7 00
Arthur Wiggin, masonry	4 00
Conway Supply Co., plow snow	5 00
Amos Larlee, labor	74 70

Russell Larlee, labor	45 90	
Fred Ritchie, labor	28 80	
Roswell Boutillier, labor	27 00	
John Irving, labor	95 80	
Reginald Harmon, labor	75 10	
Burnham Quint and truck	4 20	
		$ 652 50

To be reimbursed

NORTH CONWAY LIGHTING PRECINCT
Valuation $1,000,925

Appropriation		$3,350 00
Overlay		153 38
Additions		2 10
Paid Grace M. Cox, Treasurer	$3,479 30	
Discount	26 18	
	$3,505 48	$3,505 48

CONWAY VILLAGE FIRE DISTRICT
Valuation, $809,920

Appropriation		$5,185 00
Overlay		241 75
Refund		1,000 00
Additions		37 86
Paid H. C. Lovejoy, treasurer	$6,416 94	
Discounts	27 89	
Abatements	19 78	
	$6,464 61	$6,464 61

CENTER CONWAY LIGHTING PRECINCT
Valuation, $131,535

Appropriation		$ 460 00
Overlay		13 56
Paid Guy C. Mason, treasurer	$470 17	
Discount	3 39	
	$ 473 56	$ 473 56

AUDITORS' CERTIFICATE

Center Conway, N. H., Feb. 21, 1939

We hereby certify that we have this day examined the accounts of the Selectmen of Conway for the fiscal year ending January 31, 1939, and find them correct with vouchers on file for each and every item under their proper heads.

R. N. DAVIS
A. G. LORD

Auditors.

AUDITORS' CERTIFICATE

Conway, N. H., Feb. 18, 1939

We hereby certify that we have this day examined the financial accounts of Leslie C. Hill, Town Clerk, for the fiscal year ending January 31, 1939, and find them correct.

R. N. DAVIS
A. G. LORD

Auditors.

TREASURER'S REPORT

To the Auditors of the Town of Conway:

The following is a report of all money received and disbursed by me as Treasurer of the Town of Conway for the fiscal year ended January 31, 1939:

RECEIPTS

Balance on hand Jan. 31, 1938	$26,198 24
R. L. Grindle	105,008 75
Loans	60,000 00
Selectmen	14,894 81
State of N. H.	9,826 08
L. C. Hill	6,347 08
Miscellaneous	438 40
	$222,713 36

DISBURSEMENTS

As per Selectmen's orders	$203,172 46
Balance on hand Jan. 31, 1939	$ 19,540 90

DETAIL OF RECEIPTS

From R. L. Grindle, Collector:

1938 Levy:

August 6	$35,000 00
August 11	7,000 00
September 3	3,500 00
October 3	6,500 00
October 11	1,500 00
October 24	1,500 00
November 5	5,500 00
November 15	2,500 00
November 28	4,000 00
December 3	7,000 00
December 12	4,000 00
January 3, 1939	6,500 00

January 28	11,000 00	
January 31	9,500 00	
November 28, 1938, Capital		
Stock tax	75	
November 28, 1938 Capital		
Stock Tax	8 00	
		$105,008 75

Loans:

Hartford Conn. Trust Co.,		
4/23/38	40,000 00	
Lincoln R. Young, 1/20/39	20,000 00	
		$60,000 00

Miscellaneous Sources:

May 17, Town of Albany, plowing	$259 50	
May 17, Town of Madison, plowing	66 00	
Jan. 31, One-half Surveyor's bill		
Town of Bartlett—town lines	17 50	
Jan 31, Town of Bartlett, plowing	95 40	
		$ 438 40

L. C. Hill, Clerk:

1938 Auto Permits

March 5	$ 600 00	
April 2	2,400 00	
May 7	500 00	
June 4	375 03	
July 2	200 00	
August 6	1,070 00	
September 3	325 00	
October 3	100 00	
November 5	110 00	
January 7	143 36	
January 31, 1939, 38 auto permits	157 66	
Jan. 31, 1939, auto permits	134 53	
		$ 6,115 58

Dog Taxes: 1938

March 5	36	00
August 6, 1937	12	50
August 6	48	00
November 5	50	00
January 20	30	00
January 31	41	00

$217 50

August 6, Filing Fees $ 14 00

State of New Hampshire:
Reimbursement for Relief expend.

20% for January 3/31/38	$226	67
20% for February 5/11/38	211	90
20% for March 5/17/38	217	84
20% for December '37, 7/2/38	182	98
15% for May 7/21/38	113	96
15% for April, 8/6/38	245	10

$1,198 45

Miscellaneous:

Bounties	72	00
May 17 Forest fires	18	70
Jan. 14, State Forester fire bills	5	23
Jan. 14, State Forester fire bills	10	89
Jan. 31, interest	3,283	24
Jan. 31, Insurance tax	11	66
Jan. 31 Railroad tax	2,481	18
Jan. 31, Savings Bank tax	2,740	88
Jan. 31, National Forest reserve fund	2	65
Jan. 31, Unexpended Blister Rust Fund	1	20

$8,627 63

From Selectmen

March 5, 1938

Sale of Culverts to State	$ 21	42
Sale of tar, Bolduc	79	00
Refund, Blister Rust	6	00
W. L. Jackson, back tax and int.	50	93
Collector's fees, H. O. Loan Corp.	2	85
Repairs to R. R. Yard, Div. 2	122	49
Fred Pease, reimbursement	6	00
Zacker family, reimbursement	8	00
Adelaid Savard, back tax	29	18

April 2

Lydia Howard, poll tax refund	2	00
Taxes bought by town	4,489	91
Tax redeemed before tax sale	12	00
Taxes redeemed prior to sale	1,519	43
Tax sold prior to sale	163	64
Apply against 1937 item No. 4813	23	06
Interest on tax redeemed	34	34
Interest on tax redeemed	4	12
Interest on tax bought by town	112	61
Poll tax sold town	116	00
Poll tax on 1937 warrant	94	00 -
Harris Twombly, 36-37 taxes	67	48
Home Owners Loan Corp., tax	534	89
Arthur Seavey, 35-36 tax	193	16
P. L. Randall, 35-36 tax	215	90
Waldo G. Lowd, 35-37 tax	134	38
Town of Limerick, Me., poor	88	50

April 23

Perry's Garage, tax	215	58
Town of Limerick, poor	32	76

May 7

Interest on Perry's Garage tax	2	15
Back tax	5	00
Elizabeth Pierce, 1937 tax	199	65

May 11

J. E. Smith, '37 tax sold town	69	47
R. M. Ormiston, balance after abatement	20	12
Thom. Furlong, part '37 tax	10	00
Crosby Hallett, part '37 tax	4	00
Ed. French, part '37 tax	5	00
Sidney Welch, '37 tax & cost	7	19
Fred Hall, back tax	5	40
Harold Tyler, back tax	9	09
1937 Polls sold Town		
James and Delema Smith	4	00
Sidney and Amy Welch	4	00
Rupert Reed	2	00
Harold. Tyler	2	00
Frank Colbroth	2	00
Frank and Mina Lackie, '36 polls	4	00
1937 polls uncollected	44	00
Sidney Welch, int. after sale		12
H. Tyler, int. after sale		10

May 17

Mark Tripp, '35 tax	54	54
Town of Limerick, poor	83	00

June 15

Charles Hayes, forest fires	5	85
N. E. Metal Culvert, disc. invoice	1	02

August 6

James R. Johnson, '36-'37 back tax	30	00
Bolduc Theatre license	100	00
Home Owners Loan Corp., '35-'36 '37' Wm. Colbroth tax	77	25
Town of Limerick, poor	28	50
J. Kelley for Noyes Heath 1937 tax redemption	21	50
Elmer Archibald, back tax	81	90
Carroll County poor, A. Cook	5	00

Wm. Wyman, 1937 tax redemption
    by A. E. Kenison   519 05
E. Munroe, redemption sale '37
    tax   493 58
Gen. H/W Maintenance, Div. 1   108 00
Bennett Bros., circus fee   45 00
Rand, Rowell tax redemp. '35-'36 65 00
Carnival permit   40 00
Rent, Mary Hill house   10 00
R. Graves, part '37 tax   5 00
R. Graves, part '37 tax   10 00
Susan P. Green, redemp. '37 tax 203 77

September 3

Van Arnham's license   25 00
R. F. Harmon, taxes   563 16
Town of Limerick, poor   28 50

September 17

Tar sold Eastern Slope Inn   3 60

October 1

Rachel Garland, part back tax   3 70
Raymond Graves, back tax   17 65
Ira Snow, part back tax   5 00
B. Johnson, '37-'38 tax   20 10
Flora McCrove, tar sold   18 00
Highway Dept., rent road equip-
    ment   30 00
Price Carnival, permit   40 00
Francis Dow, '37 tax and int. 16 10
Rose Masse, back tax   75 97
Eastern Slope Inn, truck hire 10 00

November 5

Frank Tripp, '37 tax   16 77
Road Damage Settlements, Div. 1 100 00
Wm. McLellan, refund relief 5 00
Material refund Memorial Hos-
    pital, Div. 1   50 80

November 12

J. L. Liveley, '36 tax & int.	100 00
Wm. McLellan, refund relief	5 00
Guy Saunders, '37 tax, cost & interest	11 78

November 21

Ira Snow, '34 part tax	3 50

December 3

Town of Limerick, poor	18 00
Guy Jackson, back tax	10 00

January 7

Minta Pease, '37 tax	129 21
Guy Jackson, '37 part tax	10 00
John S. Shirley, '36 tax sale	238 07
Fires account, forester	4 32
L. C. Bolduc, town poor	77 72
Ed. Thompson, '37 tax	19 35
Ira Snow, back tax	1 50
Alfred Graves, part tax	10 00

January 13

Balance Acct. Sheahan Road tar PWA	150 00
Rachel Garland, '37 tax	3 70

January 31

Bowling Alley license, McLellan	50 00
Ivory Mason, '37 tax redemption	27 51
Chas. Brenman, tax redemption	240 43
C. B. Pond, '33 tax	31 50
L. C. Bolduc, relief reimbursement	74 18
A. L. Roberts, Est., '36 tax redemption	237 69
Rent, Mary Hill house	2 00
Ira Snow, back tax	5 00
Conway Village Fire Dist.	1,000 00
P. Pond, back tax '35	24 98
P. W. Seavey, '35 tax	39 81

C. A. Hill, axe handle sold		67
Proceeds, sale E. Harriman Mill	50	00
Lydia & Perley Eastman, '34 tax	57	00
J. E. Eastman ,'36 tax	19	10
R. Young, relief, soldiers' aid	12	00
H. S. Mudgett Est., '37 tax sale	93	43
Municipal Court	341	13

$14,894 81

Respectfully submitted,

MELLEN B. BENSON,
Treasurer.

AUDITORS' CERTIFICATE

Conway, N. H.
February 21, 1939

We hereby certify that we have this day audited the accounts of the Treasurer of the Town of Conway and find them correct per vouchers on file for all expenditures and balance on hand in Carroll County Trust Co. of $19,540.90.

ROBERT N. DAVIS
ARTHUR G. LORD
Auditors

REPORT OF THE PUBLIC LIBRARIES

REPORT OF THE CONWAY LIBRARY TRUSTEES
February 1, 1938 to January 31, 1939

Balance on hand Feb. 1, 1938	$ 112 40	
Received from the Town Treasurer	2,100 00	
Received from Gilbert Budroe	5 00	
Received from Trust Fund	10 00	
Received from all other sources	4 55	
Total receipts		$2,231 95

Expenditures

Salaries	$1,150 00	
Repairs on Library roof	62 00	
Other repairs	61 96	
Light and fuel	304 26	
Magazines	69 60	
Books	75 62	
Library supplies	60 45	
Incidentals	38 81	
Repairs on clock	10 60	
Cleaning	18 75	
Balance on hand, Feb. 1, 1939	379 90	
		$2,231 95
Eastman Fund	$951 25	
Conway Public Library Trust Fund	622 96	

CONWAY PUBLIC LIBRARY
REPORT YEAR ENDING DEC. 31, 1938
Financial Statement

Cash on hand Jan. 1, 1938,	$ 37 70	
Received:		
Fines,	114 07	

D. P. S. Rentals   97 84
Non-resident borrowers,   14 50
Gifts:
   Conway Woman's Club $13 00
   S. S. Robins   3 00

                                          16 00
All other sources   14 20

    Total receipts $294 31
  Paid:
Books $ 99 53
Books for D. P. S.   78 24
Periodicals   16 90
Supplies   19 62
Express and postage   8 60
Incidentals   3 55

    Total expenditures $ 261 64

Balance on hand Dec. 31, 1938 $ 32 67

Resources

Volumes owned Jan. 1, 1938   7224
Volumes added by purchase   63
Volumes added by D. P. S.   61
Volumes added by gift   267

    Total   7615
Deduct volumes lost or discarded   186

    Total volumes owned Dec. 31, 1938   7429

Services

	Adult	Juvenile	Total
Volumes non-fiction lent	2,324	858	3,182
Volumes fiction lent	14,692	3,495	18,187
Volumes rented, D.P.S.	879		879

Unbound periodicals lent	1,659	221	1,880
Total circulation	19,554	4,574	24,128
Reading room attendance			6686

LIBRARY REPORT

"Libraries are never finished, they must include not only the books that never die, but those that gather fresh wisdom out of the present and look further into the future." Books given by Charles Fraser, Kenneth Sten, Elverton Berry, Angelia Courtney, Gertrude Shurtleff, William Glackens, Charles Chamberlain, Robert Kennett, Harold Cloutman, Clarence E. Eastman and the Conway Woman's Club, have made the year 1938 one of progress. For half a century the friends of Conway's Libraries have been a forceful factor in giving good material to our town libraries.

On April 25, the State Library Commission sent its first Bookmobile to Carroll County. At this time seventy library-minded citizens from all sections of the State, met at the Presidential Inn to show their interest in and to give their support to, this Regional Library Service that New Hampshire was about to give. The Bookmobile has helped materially the library service at Conway, Center Conway and the branch library at East Conway.

Exhibits at the Conway Library were

April—W. P. A. Art Exhibit
August—Camera Portraits   Dorothy Jarvis
September—New Hampshire Landscapes, Sawyer Studio
October—Pencil Paintings   John Pratt Whitman

Respectfully submitted,

RUTH A. KENNETT,
Secretary,
Conway Library Trustees

REPORT OF CENTER CONWAY PUBLIC LIBRARY
For Year Ending December 31, 1938

Cash on hand Jan. 1, 1938	$ 5 01	
Fines received	4 10	
Rentals	7 30	
Total receipts		$ 16 41
Paid for incidentals	$ 1 98	
Paid for books	6 00	
Paid for supplies	2 50	
		$ 10 48
Balance on hand		$ 5 93

Resources

Books on hand January 1, 1938	3,520
Added by purchase	27
Added by fines	4
Added by gifts	2
Total volumes owned Dec. 31, 1938	3553

Circulation

Fiction	2,930
Juvenile	509
Miscellaneous	364
Magazines	790
Total circulation	4,593

GERTRUDE A. SNOW,

Librarian.

AUDITORS' CERTIFICATE

Conway, N. H., February 16, 1939

We hereby certify that we have this day examined the accounts of the Conway Library and find them correct, with cash on hand of $379.90.

R. N. DAVIS

A. G. LORD

Auditors.

REPORT OF REDSTONE PARK COMMISSIONERS

Balance on hand,	$ 4 60
Received from Town Treasurer	50 00
	$ 54 60

Paid Geo. Rancourt, Jr., labor	$ 31 00	
Craig's, hedge shears	1 85	
A. N. French, 2 loads manure	10 00	
Geo. Rancourt, gas and oil	3 00	
John Eastman, welding	75	
Eben Bottigi, labor and truck	4 00	
George Rancourt, labor	4 00	
		$54 60

GEORGE RANCOURT
E. H. BOTTIGI,
Park Commissioners.

REPORT OF THE CONWAY VILLAGE PARK ASSOCIATION

1938

March 1, cash on hand		$ 57 89
April 27, Wm. Frechette, labor	$ 3 60	
May 12, Geo. Wiggin	3 00	
May 13, A. D. Tibbetts	75	
May 26, Marten Schoonman	7 75	
August 3, Clifford Upham	19 65	
November 19, Clifford Upham	6 20	
1939		
January 26, John Broughton	50	
Interest	—	98
January 25, Received from town Treasurer		75 00
	$41 45	
Balance on hand	92 42	
	$133 87	$133 87

. In the early Spring several unusual expenditures will have to be laid out on the Park, which will take most of the cash on hand. One of the expenditures will be the rebuilding of the stone entrance which was demolished this winter by an unknown truck driver.

MINERVA C. SAWYER
E. H. CLOUTMAN
RUTH B. D. HORNE

Trustees.

AUDITORS' CERTIFICATE

Conway, N. H., Feb. 20, 1939

We certify that we have this day audited the accounts of the Conway Village Park Association and find them correct with a balance on hand of $92.42, and vouchers on file for each item.

R. N. DAVIS
A. G. LORD

Auditors.

SCHOOL DISTRICT OFFICERS

School Board
ARTHUR H. FURBER, Chairman   Term expires 1940
RALPH L. CROCKETT, Secretary   Term expires 1939
FRANK E. KENNETT   Term expires 1941

Moderator
HERBERT C. LOVEJOY   Conway

Clerk
NEIL C. CATES   North Conway

Treasurer
WILLIAM R. CARTER   North Conway

Auditors
CHARLES E. POOLE   North Conway
HERBERT C. LOVEJOY   Conway

Special Building Committee
ARTHUR H. FURBER   North Conway
RALPH L. CROCKETT   Redstone
FRANK E. KENNETT   Conway
JOHN C. BROUGHTON (resigned Dec. 21)   Conway
JOHN H. FULLER   North Conway
NOEL T. WELLMAN   Kearsarge
PERCY GARLAND   Conway Center
GEORGE A. YEATON   Conway
HERBERT C. LOVEJOY
     (appointed Jan. 2, 1939)   Conway
WILLIAM R. CARTER   North Conway

Superintendent of Schools
JOHN H. FULLER   North Conway

School Nurse
HARRIET M. CURREN   Conway

Attendance Officers
HARRY MARTIN   North Conway
R. F. HARMON   Conway

SCHOOL WARRANT

State of New Hampshire

To the Inhabitants of the School District in the Town of Conway, County of Carroll, qualified to vote in district affairs:

You are hereby notified to meet at the Town Hall in said District on Tuesday, the fourteenth day of March 1939, at two o'clock in the afternoon to act upon the following subjects:

1. To choose a Moderator for the ensuing year.
2. To choose a Clerk for the ensuing year.
3. To choose a Treasurer for the ensuing year.
4. To choose a member of the School Board for the ensuing three years.
5. To choose two Auditors for the ensuing year.
6. To see if the District will vote to make any alteration in the amount of money required to be assessed for the ensuing year for the support of public schools and the payment of the statutory obligations of the District, as determined by the school board in its annual report.
7. To see what sum of money the District will vote to raise and appropriate for insurance for the ensuing year.
8. To see what sum of money the District will vote to raise and appropriate for repairs and new equipment for the ensuing year.
9. To see if the District will vote to authorize the school board in the name of the District to contract with Fryeburg Academy for instruction of pupils from East Conway, and to see what sum of money the District will vote to raise and appropriate for the ensuing year.
10. To see if the District will vote to raise and appropriate the necessary sum of money to properly light the Center Conway school building and authorize the

school board to have it done, agreeable to a petition signed by Nellie M. Farnsworth, John I. Fuller and others.

11. To see if the District will vote to raise and appropriate the sum of four hundred and fifty dollars ($450.00) to grade and surface a driveway and grade the yard at the Shirley School in East Conway, New Hampshire, agreeable to a petition signed by Merwyn F. Woodward and others.

12. To act upon any other business that may be legally brought before this meeting.

Given under our hands this twenty-seventh day of February, 1939.

ARTHUR H. FURBER,
FRANK E. KENNETT,
RALPH L. CROCKETT,
School Board of Conway.

SCHOOL BOARD'S ESTIMATE FOR 1939-1940

School District of Conway

School Board's statement of amounts required to support public schools and meet other statutory obligations of the district for the fiscal year beginning July 1, 1939.

DETAILED STATEMENT OF EXPENDITURES

Support of Schools

	High Schools	Elementary Schools
Teachers' salaries	$15,800 00	$17,600 00
Text books	762 00	688 00
Scholars' supplies	1,000 00	688 00
Flags and appurtenances	25 00	15 00
Other expenses of instruction	250 00	100 00
Janitor Service	1,850 00	2,042 00
Fuel	1 350 00	1,320 00
Water, Light, Janitors' supplies	300 00	400 00
Minor repairs and expenses	250 00	600 00

Health Supervision (Medical Inspection)	330 00	1,320 00
Transportation of pupils	3,000 00	4,000 00

$24,917 00 + 28,773 00 = $53,690 00

Other Statutory Requirements

Salaries of District Officers (Fixed by district)	$ 370 00
Truant Officer and School Census (Fixed by District)	50 00
Superintendent's Excess Salary (Fixed by Supervisory Union)	1,288 00
Per Capita Tax (Report of State Treasurer)	1,466 00
Interest on District Debt	1 700 00
Other obligations	250 00

$6,626 00

Total amount required to meet School
Board's budget $52,188 00

ESTIMATED INCOME OF DISTRICT

Balance June 30, 1939 (estimate)	$1,500 00
State Aid (December 1939 Allotment)	3,860 00
Dog Tax (estimate)	300 00
High School Tuition Receipts (estimate)	750 00
Elementary School Tuition Receipts (estimate)	216 00

Deduct total estimated income (not
raised by taxation)   6,626 00

†Assessment required to balance School Board's
budget $52,188 00

Special Appropriation Proposed
(Articles in Warrant)

Fryeburg Academy tuition	$1,200 00
Insurance	1,250 00

$ 2 450 00

Total assessment required to cover budget
   and appropriations $54,638 00

Conway, N. H., February 24, 1939
                          ARTHUR H. FURBER
                          RALPH L. CROCKETT
                          FRANK E. KENNETT
                                              School Board

† **$5 per $1000 of equalized valuation must be raised for elementary schools to qualify for state aid. The net assessment must contain this amount in addition to funds raised
for high school maintenance and other statutory require-
ments.**
The amount of the $5 tax is $18,937.33

FINANCIAL REPORT OF CONWAY SCHOOL BOARD

FISCAL YEAR ENDING JUNE 30, 1938

RECEIPTS

Equalization fund from State	$ 3,405 32
From Selectmen, assessment March 1937	49,725 00
Dog Licenses	578 91
Elementary School tuitions	268 00
High School tuitions	1,104 00
Sale of property	41 22
Refunds	44 00
Sale of schoolhouse	750 00
Paid by other towns for nurse	194 00
Total receipts, all sources	$56,110 45
Balance on hand July 1, 1937	468 86
Grand total	$56,579 31

PAYMENTS
Administration

Salaries of officers	$ 369 00
Superintendent's salary	1,287 80

Census	12 90	
Administration	313 50	
Sub-total		$ 1,983 20

Instruction and Operation

	High	Elementary	
Teachers' salaries	$12,357 12	$15,683 50	
Text books	642 50	513 96	
Scholars' supplies	585 20	473 69	
Flags		6 45	
Other expense, instruction	307 35	117 79	
Janitor	1,250 00	2,339 00	
Fuel	166 53	1,292 84	
Water, light, and janitor supplies	350 07	372 91	
Minor repairs and expenses	606 99	752 70	
Medical inspection and health	399 00	1,921 60	
Transportation	2,629 46	4,031 16	
Fryeburg Academy tuition	882 00		
Sub-total	$20,176 22	$27,505 60	$47,681 82

Fixed Charges and Special Appropriations

Per Capita Tax	$ 1,396 00	
Insurance	673 00	
Grading at Center Conway	200 15	
New equipment	554 15	
Sub-total		$ 2,823 30
Total payments for all purposes		$52,488 32

Cash on hand $4,090 99

Grand total $56,579 31

ARTHUR H. FURBER
FRANK E. KENNETT
RALPH L. CROCKETT
School Board of Conway.

June 30, 1938

AUDITORS' CERTIFICATE

This is to certify that we have examined the books and other financial records of the School Board of Conway, of which this is a true summary for the fiscal year ending June 30, 1938, and find them correctly cast and properly vouched.

CHARLES E. POOLE
HERBERT C. LOVEJOY
Auditors of Conway School District

June 30, 1938

REPORT OF TREASURER

FISCAL YEAR ENDING JUNE 30, 1938

Cash on hand July 1, 1937	$ 468 86
Received appropriations for current year	49,725 00
Received from dog tax	578 91
Received from State Treasurer	3,405 32
Received from other sources	2,401 32
Received from all sources	$56,110 45
Less school board orders, paid	52,569 31
Balance on hand June 30, 1938	$ 4,090 31

WILLIAM R. CARTER,
Treasurer.

June 30, 1938.

AUDITORS' CERTIFICATE

This is to certify that we have examined the books, vouchers, bank statements and other financial records of the treasurer of the school district of Conway, of which the above is a true summary for the fiscal year ending June 30, 1938, and find them correct in all respects.

CHARLES E. POOLE
HERBERT C. LOVEJOY
Auditors.

June 30, 1938.

Report of Superintendent

To the School Board and the Citizens of Conway:

Because of resignations at the end of the school year last June, three new teachers were appointed to our present staff. In the high school Mr. Karl Seidenstuecker, a graduate of Dartmouth College, was appointed teacher of history and assistant coach, and Miss Hugena Dunbar, a graduate of Simmons College, was appointed to the Commerce position. The vacancy in the Shirley school at East Conway was filled by the election of Miss Ruth Banfill, a graduate of the elementary course at Keene Normal school.

During the summer the Redstone school was painted and considerable inside painting done at the high school. These were the major items in the repair program.

The increase in the school population continues. The registration in December showed an increase of about twenty-five over last year and since these statistical tables were compiled, we have had a number of admissions. The average registration exceeds that of ten years ago by about one hundred-fifty.

The North Conway school, the Redstone school, the Grammar school at Conway Center, and the Shirley School are filled to capacity. The situation at the Conway

Grammar school has been relieved by the use of the Primary building, so-called, but this building is unfit for school occupancy and will not be used after this year when the seventh and eighth grades of the grammar school will be housed in the high school addition.

The situation at North Conway is the most serious. Here we expect over 200 pupils next year and fifty or more pupils in the two upper rooms as now organized. Another teacher is needed in this school and some plan can be worked out to relieve the overcrowding.

Additional and adequate school facilities will be afforded at the high school next year. The high school addition provides for a shop for manual arts, a cooking and sewing room for household arts, a cafeteria, a science laboratory, a commerce unit for bookkeeping and typewriting, a combination auditorium and gymnasium, new class rooms and accommodations for the seventh and eighth grades of the grammar school.

In the planning of the building we have had the services of a well-known firm of architects who have had wide experience in school construction. The building committee is spending a great deal of time and effort on the project. Every detail of planning is studied with experts and decisions on design and equipment are made solely on the basis of educational utility. The result should be a modern school plant.

It is not our purpose to incorporate any part of the grammar school with the high school. These grades will have their own teacher or teachers and the same course of instruction which they now have. The so-called junior high school organization is not adapted to the situation in Conway. It is an educational hybrid and is excessively costly in small towns and cities. Whatever contribution the junior high school idea has made to education both as to method and as to content has already been utilized in our grammar school organization with the exception of the manual and household

arts.   There is ample opportunity for pupils to avail
themselves of the opportunities in the household and
manual arts during their four years in high school.

JOHN H. FULLER,

Superintendent.

February 24, 1939.

REPORT OF HEADMASTER

John H. Fuller, **Superintendent:**

The total registration in the High School to February 1st, is 223, divided as follows:

4   post graduates
44   seniors
44   juniors
61   sophomores
70   freshmen

There are 108 boys and 115 girls registered.   16
students have left school divided as follows: 4 seniors,
2 juniors, 3 sophomores, 7 freshmen; 9 boys and 7 girls
in all.   Of these, one is married, three have moved out
of town, and twelve lacked ambition, courage or ability
to do satisfactory school work of the kind offered.

The attendance record to Feb. 3 was 97.2%, an excellent record.   There had been a total of 141 tardinesses
at that time, the worst record in the history of the
school.

At mid-year the following honors were announced,
on the basis of college certificate grade, or better: 2
students in six courses, 3 in five courses, 32 in four
courses, and 22 in three courses.   No listing of honor
grades in less than three subjects has been made.   During the same period 41 pupils failed in 63 courses.   The
majority of these failures was due to lack of study both
at school and at home.   No pupil who fails to be included on the honor list should be excused from home
study.

In June, 1938, a class of 30 was graduated: 15 boys and 15 girls. Of these, two boys and two girls are attending colleges or universities; two boys and one girl are attending junior colleges, one girl is at normal school, and three girls are attending nurses' training schools, two boys and two girls are doing post graduate work at the high school level; 15 of the 30 are continuing their education.

Respectfully submitted

ELLIS W. McKEEN,

Headmaster.

REPORT OF STATE NURSE

Report of the Child Health and Toxoid Clinic held in North Conway, November 18, 1938.

Number of children having physical examinations by a doctor	42
Number of children found defective	29
Number of defects found	34
Number of children received the diphtheria immunization treatment	23

The clinic was conducted by the State Board of Health with the cooperation of the Community Health Committee.

ROSE HARKINS,

County of Carroll

State Nurse

TABLE I

Teachers and Schools—1938-1939

Kennett High School

Ellis W. McKeen, Headmaster, Mathematics
Samuel T. Fuller, Social Science
Mabelle S. Kent, Latin and History
Clinton L. White, Sciences

Jessie Gibson, English
Helen L. Dean, French and English
Karl Seidenstuecker, History and Science
Hugena M. Dunbar, Commerce

Total registration	215
Number of tuition pupils	22

Conway Grammar School

	Teacher	Number of Pupils
Grades 6, 7 & 8	Irvin H. Gordon, Principal	73
	Charlotte Floyd, Assistant	
Grade 5	Madeline Whitcomb	32
Grade 4	Dorothea Ward	24
Grade 3	Frances Holt	29
Grade 2	Helen Cotton	27
Grade 1	Lillian Connolly	31

North Conway Grammar School

	Teacher	Number of Pupils
Grades 7 & 8	James Armstrong, Principal	42
Grades 5 & 6	Bertha F. James	45
Grades 3 & 4	Mary Skill	39
Grades 2 & 3	Hazel Maxim	38
Grade 1	Myrtle W. Gosselin	27

Conway Center Grammar School

	Teacher	Number of Pupils
Grades 5 - 8	Nellie M. Farnsworth, Principal	28
Grades 1 - 4	Dorothy M. Sherry	24

One-Room Schools

	Teacher	Number of Pupils
Redstone	Marion Young	36
West Side	Kathryn B. Sargent	30
Shirley	Ruth Banfill	29
Total elementary pupils		554
Total high school pupils		215

Total all schools	769

TABLE II
Statistics School Year 1937-1938
Schools arranged in order of attendance records.

School	Pupils	Percent Attendance	Tardy	Supt. Visits
Conway, 3 & 4	25	97.7	15	54
West Side	38	97.0	8	30
North 7 & 8	34	96.6	51	41
Conway 5	26	96.2	31	41
Kennett	207	95.8	178	48
North 5 & 6	44	95.6	6	19
Conway 2	36	95.4	10	48
North 2 & 3	37	94.7	23	18
Conway 1	31	94.5	17	17
Conway 6	26	94.4	27	40
Conway 7 & 8	51	94.4	44	47
North 3 & 4	36	94.0	28	29
Center 5 - 8	26	94.0	78	34
East	31	94.0	67	23
Conway 3	24	93.4	4	13
North 1	31	91.5	55	27
Redstone	34	91.5	113	48
Center 1 - 4	33	90.3	48	30
Totals	770		803	607

Percentage attendance, all schools, 95.1
Non-resident elemetary pupils, 8
Non-resident high school pupils, 17
Pupills transported, 189

TABLE III

Medical Inspection, Year Ending June 30, 1938
Examiners: Dr. C. M. Wiggin, Dr. J. Z. Shedd.
School nurse: Harriet M. Curren, R.N.
Pupils examined: 744; Teachers: 1

	Number of Defects	Corrections Since 1937
Vision	7	36
Hearing	1	

Cardiac disease	4	
Teeth	122	520
Tonsils	47	15
Breathing	1	
Adenoids	20	
Enlarged glands	9	20
Hard wax	15	

Dental clinics were held at the offices of Drs. Mackay, Matus and Reynolds. Contributions were received from the North Conway Woman's Club, the Red Cross and the North Conway Parent-Teachers Association. Eye clinics were held at the office of J. P. Carter and at the Eye and Ear Infirmary at Portland.

REPORT OF THE TRUST FUNDS OF THE TOWN OF CON W, N. H., JANUARY 31, 1939.

Date of Creation	Trust Funds—Purpose of Creation	How Invested	Amount of Principal	Rate of Interest	Balance of Income on hand at beginning of year	Income During year	Expended During year	Balance of Income on hand at end of year
? 2, 1908	Andrew Dinsmore Cemetery Trust Fund.	Nh On way lan & Banking	150.00	2¼%	90.45	5.43	5.00	9 0.88
May 9, 1912	Conway ... Od Mary Trust Fund. Cline W. Mill and ... thrs rd.	North lan & Banking	290.00	2¼%	187.23	9.66	1.00	146.89
Jan. 1, 1917	... Smith ... Fund. r18th dr.	Nh lan & Banking	50.00	2¼%	10.93	1.36	1.00	11.29
June 4, 1920	Mary Adjutant Cemetery Fund.	Nh lan & Banking	100.00	2¼%	13.82	2.56	5.00	11.38
April 3, 1922	Mary Banfill School Fund. Banfill dr.	Nh ... Loan & Banking	285.00	2¼%	11.94	5.58		17.52
Aug. 16, 1922	Osgood, ... ad Emerson ... J. Fred ... thrs donors.	Carroll County Trust	40.00	2¼%	35.82	9.85	8.00	37.67
Feb. 3, 1923	West Side ... Fund. Frank P. Allard and others	Nh lan & Banking	693.21	2¼%	62.23	17.08	1 5.00	64.31
Jan. 2, 1925	... Hill ... Care of ... and lot. ... of Conway donor.	Nh lan & Banking	85.79	2¼%	6.10	2.07	2.00	6.17
June 5, 1925	Winifred ... Fund. ... donor.	Carroll County Fund.	20.00	2¼%	60.15	5.88	5.00	61.03
July 2, 1925	Brooks ... Fund. E. H. Brooks donor.	North Conway Loan & Banking Company	20.00	2¼%	63.80	5.96	3.00	66.76
May 19, 1926	... P. ... Fund. Deering Cemetery. Emma P. Atkinson, donor.	City Trust	100.00	2¼%	12.61	2.54		15.15
?, 1927	Charlotte Meserve Cemetery Fund. dr.	North Conway lan & Banking	30.00	2¼%	62.28	8.19	8.00	62.47
?, 1927	... Fund. Emma N. Cook, dr.	North lan & Banking	150.00	2¼%	8.43	3.59	2.50	9.52
Feb. 23, 1928	Etta ... Fund. Etta Tarr, donor.	Carroll County Trust	30.00	2¼%	55.31	8.03	5.00	58.34

Trust Funds Continued

Date	Fund / Donor	Bank	Principal	Rate				Total
Sept. 24, 1928	Sarah J. Carter Cemetery Fund. Sarah J. Carter donor.	North Conway Loan & Banking Company	100.00	2¼%	35.57	3.06		38.63
July 10, 1929	Julia Webster Cemetery Fund. Julia Webster donor.	Carroll County Trust Company	100.00	2¼%	30.09	2.93		33.02
Aug. 20, 1929	Charles J. and Alice R. Snow Cemetery Fund. Charles J. and Alice R. Snow donors.	Carroll County Trust Company	100.00	2¼%	29.70	2.92		32.62
July 19, 1932	Calhoun Cemetery Fund. George W. Calhoun donor.	Carroll County Trust Company	310.83	2¼%	51.59	8.18		59.77
Nov. 29, 1932	Robertson Cemetery Fund. Emeline Fullerton donor.	Carroll County Trust Company	100.00	2¼%	1.39	2.28	2.25	1.42
Dec. 2, 1932	Garland Cemetery Fund. Susie M. Ham and Hannah A. Garland donors.	Carroll County Trust Company	100.00	2¼%	14.92	2.58		17.50
Dec. 5, 1933	Ann R. Russell Cemetery Fund. Ann R. Russell donor.	Carroll County Trust Company	500.00	2¼%	47.04	12.37	5.00	54.41
Sept. 5, 1934	Richard B. Thorn Cemetery Fund. Mrs. Martha Susan Hale Shackford Thorn donor	Carroll County Trust Company	194.66	2¼%	16.60	4.77		21.37
Sept. 5, 1934	Samuel B. Shackford Cemetery Fund. Heirs of Samuel B. Shackford donors	Carroll County Trust Company	100.00	2¼%	3.45	2.33	2.50	3.28
July 30, 1935	Samuel C. Hatch Cemetery Fund. Susan F. Morton, donor.	Carroll County Trust Company	100.00	2¼%	6.16	2.39		8.55
Dec. 16, 1935	Lucia Morrill Lougee Cemetery Fund. Care of Morrill Cemetery. Lucia Morrill Lougee, donor.	Carroll County Trust Company	150.00	2¼%	7.61	3.55		11.16
June 18, 1936	Roy W. Hill Cemetery Fund. Mr. and Mrs. Roy W. Hill, Donors.	Carroll County Trust Company	100.00	2¼%	3.78	2.34		6.12
June 18, 1936	Francis L. Hazelton Cemetery Fund. Winifred C. Cole, Donor.	Carroll County Trust Company	100.00	2¼%	3.78	2.34		6.12
Nov. 9, 1936	Bemis—Taylor Cemetery Fund. Arthur S. Taylor and Alberta F. Titcomb, Donors.	Carroll County Trust Company	100.00	2¼%	.72	2.26	2.00	.98
June 24, 1938	Curtis Sinclair Cemetery Fund. Ellen H. Davis and others donors.	Carroll County Trust Company	300.00	2%		3.00		3.00

LESLIE C. HILL, ROBERT H. KENNETT, CHARLES E. POOLE, Trustees Trust Funds, Conway, N. H.

VITAL STATISTICS

TO THE SELECTMEN—in compliance with an act of Legislature passed June session 1887, requiring clerks of towns and cities to furnish a transcript of the record of births, marriages, and deaths to the municipal officers for publication in the Annual Report, I hereby submit the following:

Births Registered in the Town of Conway, N. H., for the Year Ending December 31, 1938.

Date of Birth	Name of Child	No. of Child 1st, 2nd, &c.	Name of Father	Maiden Name of Mother	Birthplace of Father	Birthplace of Mother
Jan. 1	David James		Joseph Ralph Therrien	Esther A. Turgeon	Berlin	Conway
8	Newell Libuis, Jr.		Newell L. Frost	Phyllis M. Dow	Madison	Farmington
12	Paula Joan		Kermit R. Horne	Doris C. Burke	Milan	Bartlett
15	William Wendell		Maurice W. Leavitt	Dora V. Heald	Madison	Lawrence, Mass.
22	Evelyn Ann		Harold E. Shaw	Eleanor F. Whitman	Moultonboro	Chelsea, Mass.
28	Crosby Coleman		Crosby Hallett	Emily Hartford	Albany	Maynard, Mass.
30	William Norman		Norman Brackett	Emily McKeen	Conway	Easton, Mass.
31	Robert		Robert Bean	Barbara B. Downs		Albany
31	Shirley Elaine		Philip A. Allen	Evelyn A. Mason	Conway	Redstone
Feb. 8	Glendon Maurice		Charles H. Brosnan	Florence Willey	Berwick, Me.	Conway
18	Sally Ann		Bernard L. Clark	Bernice Chase	Conway	Conway
19	Norman Dale		Harold E. Ellis	Martha M. Taplin	Snowville	Lawrence, Mass.
21	Barbara Mae		Robert J. O'Leary, Jr.	Cora Robinson	Portland, Me.	Machias, Me.
21	Ralph Eugene, Jr.		Ralph E. Roberts	Gladys M. Nute	Bartlett	Bartlett
24	Nancy Anne		Carroll A. Hill	Dorothy Roberts	Conway	Boston, Mass.
25	John Carl		Charles S. Hill	Arlene Webster	Farmington	Conway
27	Jacqueline		Stewart Dudley	Ruth Farnham	Derry	Conway
28	Sandra Wanda		Harry S. Ellis, Jr.	Doris M. Nelson	Snowville	Madison
Mar. 1	Norman Fred		Russell V. Webster	Albina Lella Allard	Somerville, Mass.	Newfield, Me.
1	Janet Potter		Clarence H. Davidson	Hazel B. Potter	Conway	Conway
6			Robert W. Chandler	Lilah A. Garland		Jackson
9	Alton Merle, Jr.		Alton M. Hurd	Helen Ethel Gilman	Madison	Chocorua
13	Virginia Irene		David L. Baker	Jessie M. Shackford	Portland, Me.	Madison
19	Robert Eugene		Albert E. Lloyd	Marie C. Lusk	Somerville, Mass.	Cambridge, Mass.
19	John Truman		George E. Thurston	Myrtle Twitchell	Conway	Lewiston, Me.
24	Franklin James		John L. Brown	Edvie A. Thurston	Albany	Effingham
25	Mary Ann		James McGreal	Bridie McGrath	Ireland	Ireland

Births Continued

Month	Day	Name	Father	Residence	Mother	Residence
	29	Cheryl Elizabeth	Roland L. Morse	Willimantic, Conn.	Constance L. Walker	Intervale
	30	Claire Frances	Noyes K. Heath	Fryeburg, Me.	Dorothy F. Harring	Boston, Mass.
	30	Mary Grace	Mark Nickerson	Madison	Reva Chapman	Brownfield, Me.
April	1	Eloise Louise	Elwood L. Henry	Bartlett	Ethel M. Chase	Lancaster
	5	Leo George, Jr.	Leo G. Roux	Laconia	Irja L. Schroderus	Norway, Me.
	9	Philip	Clinton W. Trussell	Belmont	Rose L. Coleman	Concord
	9	Phyllis	Clinton W. Trussell	Belmont	Rose L. Coleman	Concord
	10	Lois Ruth	Archibald Allen	Glen	Elsie M. Neally	Bartlett
	21	Carl Stanley	Stanley Hunter	Redstone	George Parker	Portland, Me.
	29	Arthur Malcolm	Hibbert A. Warner	Canada	Ardis M. Fales	Canada
	30	Fay Patricia	Walter E. Scott	Canada	Gladys I. Clark	Winterport, Me.
May	3	Roberta Eleanor	Everett M. Wiggin	Conway	Clara M. Budroe	Conway
	5	Frances Anne	John E. Coghlan	Malone, N. Y.	Ethel A. Lawrence	Montpelier, Vt.
	7	Frances Anne	Frank P. Helphard	Portland, Me.	Annie P. Munroe	Effingham
	14	Gloria Lee	George H. Gardner	Bartlett	Priscilla R. Eastman	Winchester
	15	Constance	Arthur B. Callan	Worcester, Mass.	Mary A. Bernier	Norwood, Mass.
	18	Richard Albert	Charles E. Davidson	Conway	Edna Fernald	Bartlett
	21	Harold Kenneth	Harold W. Barbour	Brookline	Mildred H. Jackson	Boston, Mass.
	31	Brian Ashton	Edward B. Knight	Conway	Sophie Berzin	Brockton, Mass.
June	5	Nancy Jane	Austin D. Savary	Albany	Violet A. Hulet	Landsgrove, Vt.
	6	Harry Neal	Harry S. Seavey	Conway	Beulah M. MacDonald	Lowell, Mass.
	10	Infant	Raymond W. Parish	Canada	Katherine Campbell	Calais, Me.
	14	Dolores Armstrong	James H. Armstrong	Grafton	Marguerite Eastman	Conway
	20	June Bernice	Leo E. Treadwell	Springfield, Me.	Mabel E. Lenard	Andover, Me.
	24	Dorothy Elizabeth	Charles E. Dodge	New London	Dorothy Smith	Pittsfield
	11		Kenneth Winslow		Elizabeth Gallagher	
July	6	Carol Ann	Harold G. Hill	Tamworth	Dorothy I. Milliken	Westboro, Mass.
	6	Jacqueline Marie	Frank E. Drew	Conway	Phylis A. Grendell	Chapman, Me.
	7	Henry Ellsworth	George H. Brooks	Conway	Barbara F. Hill	Bartlett
	12	Jeanette Ruth	Milton W. Boothby	Conway	Ruth Howe	Roxbury, Mass.
	20	James Wilbur	George A. Conrad	Canada	Gladys R. Marston	Passaconaway
	20	Karl Whitman	John B. Oliver	Boston, Mass.	Leila A. Parmiter	Minetto, N. Y.
	21	Harriet Loretta	Paul R. Harriman	Wolfeboro	Mary J. Burke	Lynn
	27	Dorothy Marie	Gordon M. Towle	Silver Lake	Myrtle A. Colbroth	Conway
	28	Clifford Austin, Jr.	Clifford A. Milliken	Freedom	Irene Boucher	New Durham
	29	Donna Ann	Donald E. Potter	Fryeburg, Me.	Gertrude Nickerson	Limington. Me.
	30	Lorothy Alice	Earl W. Chandler	Bartlett	Sellma G. Kennedy	Quincy, Mass.
Aug.	3	Sally Ann	William H. McGrath	Harrisville	Louise E. Douglass	Gorham
	3	John White	Herman D. Edgerly	Chocorua	Natalie N. White	Ossipee
	4	Henry Hoadley, 3rd	Henry H. Guernsey, Jr.	Edensburg, Penn.	Faustina M. M. Reed	Woolwich, Me.
	6	Jacqueline Lee	Leon I. Howard	Jackson	Lillian K. Dearborn	Glen
	9	Maxine Alice	Max J. Weld	Sandwich	Pauline Gessner	Jefferson

No.					
10	Anna Shirley	Howard A. Johnston	Hilda S. Shirley	Derry	Woodland, Me.
16	Blaine Malcolm	William McLellan, Jr.	Helen M. Tupin	Conway	Lawrence, Mass.
21	Patrick Allan	Willis R. Twombly	Helen Shanahan	Conway	Lynn, Mass.
30	Carol Ann	Carroll G. Whitaker	Anita L. Paradis	Conway	Mexico, Me.
31	Edward Francis	Leo Morissette	Laura M. Berry	Island Pond, Vt.	Woolmoro, Vt.
4	Ann	Francis R. Conway	Marion B. Bonn	Dexter, Me.	Buxton
10	Virginia Charlotte	Terry R. Garland	Emma Fox	Conway	Porter, Me.
11	Carroll Herman	Lewis Derboski	Florence Robucks	Middlebury, Vt.	Ludlow, Vt.
18	Jon Adam Phillips	Herman G. Warren	Mary L. Sanborn	Denmark, Me.	Bridgton, Me.
18	Sylvia Ann	Walter G. Munro	Louisa Thurston	Conway	Boston, Mass.
18	Dunn	Kenneth G. Wiggin	Theodora Manthorn	Coppenll, Mass.	Conway
19	Gordon Conran	Wendell A. Leon	Jean B. Marsh	Quincy, Mass.	Arlington, Mass
20	Fay Marie	Edmund F. Moton	Clara V. St. John	Havana, Mass.	Bull River, Mi
24	Loraine Alma	Charles B. Birch	Blanch G. Frye	Conway	Conway
25	baby girl	Philip L. Perry	Evelyn B. Morrill	Alton	Sherburn, Vt.
27	Kenneth Rodney	Warner G. Dearden	Anna V. Gallagher	Lynn, Mass.	Boston, Mass.
5	Mary Louise	Herbert B. Pront	Ruth Harmon	Conway	Mandbll, Me.
10	Harley Alfred	William H. Dillingor	Alice L. Winn	Lowell, Me.	Windsor, Vt.
12	Harvey Frank	Howard G. Davis	Caroline Thrift	Fenton, Me.	Iowa Brook,
17	Margaret Pearl	Frank B. Garland	Muriel M. Clark	Tamworth	Harrington
19	Harold Irving	Forrest W. Johnson	Effie P. Bonn	Tamworth	Tamworth
20	Gary Wilson	Harold L. Potter	Irene V. Lane	Pryburg, Me.	Liverman
24	Tomita Ethel	Edward F. Dolly	Alma M. Marsun	So. Portland, Me.	Denmark, Me.
25	David Guy	Frank T. Longue	Vera Wiggin	Lynn, Mass.	Conway
28	Patricia Ann	John R. Fox	Ruth R. Holt	Paris, Me.	Lovell, Me.
28	Lola Elaine	William H. Fagan	Helen R. Cholbroth	Harrison, Me.	Portland, Me.
4	David Reid	Wilbur Robertson	Helma Davis	Canada	Hebron
5	Stanley Almon	Marie R. Kennett	Doris L. MacKenna	Madison	Boston, Mass.
6	Carol Mae	Oliver T. Charles	Leona G. Reid	Jackson	Gorham
18	Virginia Marie	Arthur K. Crossey	Reba M. Manchester	Westbrook, Me.	Windham, Me.
20	Richard Morton	Ashley J. Webster	Ruby Dunfro	Gustine, Me.	Milo, Me.
27	Florence Irene	Laurin E. Willey	Ruth G. Jewell	Bridgton, Me.	Conway
28	Joseph Edward	Frank B. Bryant	Arlene R. Whitney	Passamaonnway.	Portland, Me.
28	Margaret Olive	Philip J. Holden	Dolly W. Jackson	Boston, Mass.	Conway
1	Donald Ray	Louis F. Hobart	Constance J. Cruce	Glen	Port McKinley
7	Lynda Louise	Ivan T. Taylor	Myrtle R. Moody	Jackson	Lebanon
7	Reginald Lombard	Abbott A. Gardner	Dorothy A. Bushman	Sweden, Me.	Conway
9	Don Kenrick	Henry W. Mann	Lesbe E. Garland	Brownfield, Mo.	Tamworth
11	Ann Mellette	Leon H. Chick	Velma L. Tombard	St. Paul, Minn.	Lynn, Me.
11	Donald Louis	Byan K. Saunders	Joyce Kennedy	Madison	St. Paul, Minn
		L. Raymond Ambrose	Tilmey G. Player	Boston, Mass.	Turbeyville, N.
		Wallace T. Smphy	Pauline Chappen		Bartlett

13	... Lawrence	Bertrand F. ...	Mae E. ...	Conway	Waterford, Me.
14	Ann Cousens	D. ... Davidson	Florence Cousens	...	...
19	Janet ...	Herbert W. Burke	Anna B. Colbroth	Ashland, Me. ...	Clarendon, Vt.
25	...	Don ... Pls	Lottle Demsha	...	stonB Mass.
30	ohn Curtis, Jr.	ohn C. ...	Frances S. Willey	New ...	...

Marriages Recorded in the Town of Conway, N. H., for the Year ending December 31, 1938.

Date	Place of Marriage	Name and Surname of Groom and Bride	Residence of Each at Time of Marriage	Age of Each	Place of Birth of Each	Name, Official Station of Person by Whom Married
Jan. 1		Herbert J. ...	Conway	26	Bristol, Me.	H. Olsen, C
1		Mildred E. ...	Conway	22	Conway	
		By W. Merrow	Conway	20	Conway	C. H. ...
		Joe H. ...	Conway	20	Conway	Berlin
2		... H. Davis	Norway, Me.	36	Fryeburg, Me.	L. C Hill, J.P.
		Mildred Wilson	Auburn, Me.	34	Mechanic Falls, Me.	
3		Leonard M. Brann	Orono, Me.	20	Jefferson, Me.	H. Raymond Phelts, C.
		Harriet Robie	Orono, Me.	19	Portland, Me.	
Feb. 5		Herbert B. McKenney	South Portland Me.	29	South Portland, Me.	J. G. P. Sherburne. C.
		... E. L. Huff	Scarboro, Me.	44	Scarboro, Me.	
9		Frank E. Littlefield	Conway	42	Bartlett	L. C Hill, J.P.
		... J. Currier	Conway	29		
14		Wilson F. ...	Portland, Me.	22	Portland, Me.	L. C Hill, J.P.
		Beverly H. Springer	South Portland, Me.	21	Portland, Me.	
26		Forrest E. Richardson	Boston, Mass.	40	Eastbrook, Me.	L. C Hill, J.P.
		Phyllis ...	stonB ...	33	Isleboro, Me.	
Mar. 12		M. Parker Allen	... Me.	23	... Me.	L. C Hill, J.P.
		Juanita E. Beals	Jonesport, Me.	21	Jonesport, Me.	
15		Freeman A. Howard	... Me.	26	Hiram, Me.	L. C. ...
		Martha C. Hilton	Denmark, Me.	22	... Me.	
19		... G. Douglass	... Me.	24	Bridgton, Me.	L. C. ...
		... D. DeCoteau	Norway, Me.	19	Norway, Me.	
21		C. Robert Fall	Conway	22	Brownfield, Me.	L. C Hill, J.P.
		... K. Fall	Conway	33	Conway	

Date	Name	Residence	Age	Birthplace	Married by	Where married
Apr. 24	Glenn E. Gray	Conway	23	Bartlett	H. Raymond Phelps, C.	Conway
	Anna M. Boody	Waltham, Mass.	23	Dorchester, Mass.		
14	Rupert E. Russell	Bridgton, Me.	32	Harrison, Me.	L. C. Hill, J.P.	Conway
	Elizabeth H. Wright	Bridgton, Me.	24	Somerville, Mass.		
23	Elmer V. Knowles	Stratton, Me.	21	Stratton, Me.	N. M. Hill, J.P.	Conway
	June E. Lord	Oxford, Me.	20	Oxford, Me.		
May 1	Arthur J. Andrews	Fryeburg, Me.	51	Conway	L. C. Hill, J.P.	Conway
	Caroline M. Harring	Fryeburg, Me.	40	Waterville, Me.		
14	James E. Kelley	Stow, Me.	18	Conway	L. C. Hill, J.P.	Conway
	Celia M. Hodsdon	Conway	18	Sweden, Me.		
15	Herbert C. Willey	Conway	21	Conway	C. H. Moorhouse, C.	Conway
	Dorothy M. Mason	Conway	24	Brownfield, Me.		
27	Asiel G. Bennett	Conway	38	Plymouth, Me.	L. C. Hill, J.P.	Conway
	Gladys L. Givens	Conway	39	Farmington, Me.		
28	Victor F. Brown	Bridgton, Me.	41	Bridgton, Me.	L. C. Hill, J.P.	Conway
	Ethel M. Peterson	Bridgton, Me.	40	Bridgton, Me.		
28	Frederick W. Meister	Otisfield, Me.	63	Webster, Me.	L. C. Hill, J.P.	Conway
	Amy A. Losier	Otisfield, Me.	39	Norway, Me.		
June 1	Clarence H. Hamilton	Gray, Me.	39	Portland, Me.	L. C. Hill, J.P.	Conway
	Thirza M. Colley	Gray, Me.	44	Hiram, Me.		
5	Harry Dan Noel	Fryeburg, Me.	35	Colebrook	Frank Kirkpatrick, C.	Bartlett
	Geneva P. Garnett	Conway	23	Conway		
6	Daniel P. Curtin	Arlington, Mass.	28	Arlington, Mass.	J. E. Belford, R.C.P.	Conway
	Eleanor M. Foley	Waltham, Mass.	26	Somerville, Mass.		
11	Russell L. Rix	Conway	47	Berlin,	L. C. Hill, J.P.	Conway
	Harriet Merrill	Derry	51	New York City		
25	Felix J. Lavley	Conway	46	Colebrook	L. C. Hill, J.P.	Conway
	Josephine Boothby	Conway	33	South Portland, Me.		
29	Harris M. Thurston	Conway	49	Eaton	H. W. Curtis	Portsmouth
	Elizabeth Emery	Bartlett	34	Steep Falls, Me.		
July 1	Lawrence A. Garland	Conway	21	Bartlett	A. E. Lloyd, C.	Conway
	Anna M. Lein	Conway	26	Manchester		
2	Abraham Covin	Brookline, Mass.	41	Boston, Mass.	C. H. Moorhouse, C.	Conway
	Marion D. Porter	Brighton, Mass.	34	Boston, Mass.		
9	Harry L. Gothro	Portland, Me.	30	Portland, Me.	L. C. Hill, J.P.	Conway
	Amanda E. Bridge	Conway	28	Swans Island, Me.		
23	Lincoln H. Clark	Chicago, Ill.	27	New Rochelle, N. Y.	B. M. Washburn, C.	Bretton Woods, N. H.
	Alice L. Hardenbergh	Minneapolis, Minn.	27	Minneapolis, Minn.		
24	Carroll Whitaker	Conway	21	Conway	J. A. Nichols, C.	Casco, Me.
	Anita Paradis	Conway	17	Mexico, Me.		
25	Arthur A. Greene, Jr.	Conway	23	Washburn, Me.	B. W. Roberts, J.P.	White River, Jct., Vt.
	Geraldine Giles	Brownfield, Me.	26	Brownfield, Me.		

Date	Names	Residence	Residence	Age	Officiant	Place
30	Mary E.		Princeton, N. J.	37	W. T.	Me, C. Somerville, Ms.
30	his C.		Princeton, N. J.	26		
Aug. 6	Shirl E. Sproul		sma, Me.	28	L. C. Hill, J.P.	Conway
	Ethel M. Buswell		ma, Me.	25		
9	Arthur F. St ker o		Everett, Ms.	42	L. C. Hill, J.P.	Conway
	Elizabeth Lawson		Everett, Ms.	48		
13	George R. Shaw		Raymond, Me.	61	C. H.	Me. C.
	Janet S. Morgan		rd, Mo	61		
17	Everett W.			29	C. H.	Me. C.
	Bernice M. Parker			33		
18	Raeburn V. Min		New York City	24	L. C. Hill, J.P.	Conway
	Ele		New York City	16		
18	Langdon I. Garrison		Concord	27	C. H.	Me. C.
19	Franklin J.		Conway	21	L. C. Hill, J.P.	Conway
	Mildred M.		Conway	20		
25	Stanley L.		Mc Falls, Me.	29	N. M. Hill, J.P.	Me. C.
27	James W. A. Jordan		Canton, Me.	42	L. C. Hill, J.P.	Conway
	Dorothy V. Bruns		Portland, Me.	48		
31	in F. Ms., Jr.		Portland, Me.	25	H. Raymond Phelts, C.	Conway
Sept. 1	Geraldine L.	ide, Me.	Manarda, Me.	26	L. C. Hill, J.P.	Conway
	Philip J. Clement	ide, Me.	nd	25		
2	Cl ra L. Holbrook		Gorham, Me.	38	L. C. Hill, J.P.	Conway
	Lawrence Strout		Corinna, Me.	34		
9	Francis Booth		Lancaster	26	H. G. Hennon. R.C.P.	Littleton
	Baul E. Smith		Conway	36		
14	Gertrude H. Major		Bridgton, Me.	26	L. C. Hill, J.P.	Conway
	Donald K. Ridlon		Bridgton, Me.	20		
15	rt C. Drowns		Bartlett	23	F.	k, C. Bartlett
	Al fed R. Mallett			19		
18	Helen B. Crouse		Conway	21	L. C. Hill, J.P.	Conway
	Orra B. Parker		Norway, Me.	21		
19	Winona A. Oliver		Norway, Me.	24	L. C. Hill, J.P.	Conway
	Min Guptill		Jackson	20		
19	Mildred Wiggin		Conway	16	L. C. Hill, J.P.	Conway
	Gil P.		South Portland, Me.	30		
20	Faye C.		Rockland, Me.	23	H. R. Phelts, C.	Conway
	George A. Dutch		Brewer, Me.	29		
	Doris Robinson		Brewer, Me.	25		

Date		Names		Residence	Age		Officiant
25		Bernard		Conway	29		A. E.
Oct. 1					20		T. A.
		A.			40		L. C. Hill, J.P.
15		I. Bradley		Me.	27		L. C. Hill, J.P.
17		R. Bailey		Me.	24	Me.	J. G. P. Sherburne, C.
		na A. Bailey			32	Me.	
18		Robert P.		Me Falls, Vt.	20	Vt.	L. C. Hill, J.P.
		E. Mill			18		L. C. Hill, J.P.
29		B. Patterson		Boston,	21		H. D. Gasson, C.
		C.			20		
		J. Richard			21		H. R.
		L.			19		
Nov. 8					33		S. R. Savage, J.P.
		Zel na		Conway	29		Bloomfield, Vt.
12		Clifton E. Roberts			43	Vt.	C. H.
24		Alice V.			38		H. R. Phelts, C.
		R.		St.	26	Baldwin, Me.	
28		W. Hill			31		L. C. Hill, J.P.
		lyn C.		Saco, Me.	30	Biddeford, Me.	L. C. Hill, J.P.
Dec. 9		W. W.		Saco, Me.	23	Me.	J. E. Belford, R.C.P.
		D.			19	Me.	
24		Daniel K. Libby			22	Me.	
		R.		Conway	22		
28		F.		Conway	36	Italy	
		M. Barnes		Standish, Me.	21	Bradford, Penn.	L. C. Hill, J.P.
31		Benjamin A. Dow		Me.	27	Me.	
		Ethel L.			25		C. H.
31		A.			26		

Bths ― ？ in the Town of ？ay, N. H., for the Year Ending ？r 31, 1938.

Date of Death	Name of ...	Age Years	Months	Days	Place of Birth	Name of ...	Maiden Name of Mother
Jan. 1	... M. ...	58	1	17	M. Desert ... Me.	... W.	Geo. S.
4	... W. Chesley	39	4	9	Lowell, Mass.	... W.	May J.
20	... M. ...	75	11	28	Scotland	Mo.	...es V. Griffin
22	... A. E. ... Me	72	10	22	...	...	...
23	... F. ...	68	2	22	... Me.	... W.	...
28	...es E. ...	54	7	18	...	...	...
Feb. 29	Frank S. ...	62	11	13	...	... My	...
5	...e M. Shirley	66	4	22	...	Wd H. Bean	...
8	... W. Bean	60	9	13	...	... D.	Adelia Dinsmore
18	... N. ...	76	11	4	...	...	...e A. Littl field
25	... A. Bryant	26	8	27	...	...ley A. Bryant	...y E.
Mar. 11	... T. ...	72	10	23	...	...	...e P.
15	Ronald L. Merrill	1	1	17	...	... Mill	...e Brown
27	Vera M. Meserve	10	11	6	Bartlett	...s L. ... Me	...
April 15	... D. ...	56	5	16	..., Me.	...	Della Thompson
20	... R. Stern	76	3	29	Boston, Mass.	... Ster	...
May 6	...e E. Hall	78	7	25	... Me.	Solomon S. ...	Emily A.
8	... F. ...	69	10	24	...	...	...
11	...	74	3	9	...	... H. Stuart	...a Sawyer
11	Alden W. ...	78	1	6	...	J. ...	Ethel A.
16	Seth Berry	79	4	15	...	...b H. Berry	...
28	... C. ...	49	11	24	...	... C. Davis	Geo H.
de 4	... F. ...	85	4	5	...	...	...
10	...	85	3	15	...	...	Betsy
17	... L. ...	85	3	1	New ...	...	...
28	E. Irene ...	54	7	30	...	Simon J. ...	Marjory
July 7	... A. C. ...	81	7	22	...	...	...
15	Philip J. ...de Salvio	29	4	9	Italy	...e J. Bolduc	... Boutin
15	...de Salvio	65		2	..., N. Y.	Mo de Salvio	...
17	... M. Burns	77	3	16	Bartlett	... Burns	Alice Byrne
20	Samuel C. ...	55	7	20	...	...el D. ... Me	... Drown
23	... A. ...	40	8	3	...	... W.	... L.
25	G. ...	1		12	...	...e H. ...	... E.

Deaths Continued

Month	Day	Name	Yrs.	Mos.	Das.	Place	Father	Mother
Aug.	2	Izette D. Thomas	90	8	29	Burke, Vt.	John M. Eggleston	Harriet Allen
	6	John M. Dinsmore	70	4	14	Jackson	Elisha Dinsmore	Luraetta Avery
	6	Elizabeth E. Butler	74	2	13	Conway	Daniel E. Smith	Emma E. Dolloff
	8	Emma R. Ferren	81	2		Madison	John G. Ferren	Melissa Harmon
	21	Patrick A. Twombly			28	Conway	W. Raymond Twombly	Helen D. Shanahan
Sept.	24	Oliver P. Emerson	93	3	19	Hawaiian Isles	John S. Emerson	Ursula Newell
	10	Attilio Varisco	60	3	21	Italy	Edward Varisco	Guisepina Calzani
	16	John S. Waterman	39	1	11	Buxton, Me.	John N. Waterman	Ida Sheehy
	22	Bernise E. Davidson	49	7	17	North Jay, Me.	Stephen H. Morse	Orinda Richardson
	27	Bert H. Grant	43		2	Whitefield	Nelson P. Grant	Myrtie Colby
	27	Infant Dearden				Conway	Warner C. Dearden	Anna V. Gallagher
Oct.	5	Mary E. Gale		7	11	Ossipee	Parkman D. Gale	Lucille M. Gray
	5	Mary E. Odel	78	5	6	Randolph, Me.	Adniran Townsen	Emeline Weed
	9	Oscar J. Patch	37	8	21	Stannard, Vt.	Laban J. Patch	Mary E. Johnson
	9	Zilah B. Sand	73	2		Bartlett	Andrew T. Parker	Mary Emery
	23	Thomas W. Hunter	56	4	1	Scotland	Andrew Hunter	Margaret Stevenson
	30	Norman T. Gagnon	26	8	27	Conway	Frederick Gagnon	Mathilda Pennett
	30	Nellie M. Hanson	61	4	14	Sullivan, Me.	Frank Boothby	
Nov.	6	Thomas B. Mitchell	82		10	Sweden, Me.	John A. Mitchell	Phoebe Holden
	14	Zilpha R. Mason	78	4	11	Fryeburg, Me.	Jerry Maxwell	Abbie J. Merrill
	19	Charles W. Stilphen	64	4	3	Hollis, Me.	William Stilphen	Josephine Johnstone
	23	Eugene F. Smith	65		12	Canada	Melville B. Smith	Sallie Mimmes
Dec.	12	Mary A. Murphy	84	1	12	Bartlett	Dennis M. Powell	Olive J. Boynton
	12	Annie M. King	64	10	20	Epping	John W. Chandler	Mary A. Parsley
	26	Sarah A. Thurston	83	11	26	England	Darius D. Johnson	Hannah Twombly
	26	James H. Wolger	77	9	4	Conway		Eleanor Smith
	26	Elijah W. Merrill	88	4	9		Henry Merrill	

BROUGHT HERE FOR BURIAL.

Date 1938	Place of Death	Name and Surname of the Deceased	AGE Yrs.	Mos.	Days	Place of Interment
Jan. 13	Bartlett	Caroline M. Eastman	83	7	7	Kearsarge Village Cemetery
21	Somerville, Mass.	Raymond G. Hazelton	39			Center Conway Cemetery
Feb. 8	Laconia	Rosetta C. Foss	49	2	18	Conway Village Cemetery
Mar. 2	Franklin	Helen A. Holmes	81	3	5	Kearsarge Village Cemetery
8	Eaton	Martin A. Hawkins	88	9	29	North Conway Cemetery
30	Haverhill, Mass.	Leonard A. Tilton	71	3	4	Conway Village Cemetery
May 23	Boston, Mass.	Horace F. Randall	85			Conway Village Cemetery
Aug. 1	Madison	Margaret Broadbent	39	2	17	Center Conway Cemetery
15	Augusta, Me.	Owen McNally	73	10	10	Catholic Cemetery
Sept. 22	Westboro, Mass.	Eleanor Preble	23			Conway Village Cemetery
Oct. 3	Columbus, Ohio	Laura Bickford	88			Conway Village Cemetery
10	Waterboro, Me.	Lester Mason	69	5	8	Center Conway Cemetery
28	Taunton, Mass.	Frank C. Eastman	58?			Kearsarge Village Cemetery
31	Concord	Elmer Henderson	72	8	4	Center Conway Cemetery
Nov. 24	Steuben, Me.	Addie Florence White	72	8	12	Conway Village Cemetery
24	Newburyport, Mass.	Mary E. Donovan	76			Conway Village Cemetery
29	Boston, Mass.	Everett K. Freeman	69	10		Center Conway Cemetery
Dec. 17	Albany	Addie R. Annis	66	10		Conway Village Cemetery
1915						
May 30	Eaton	Randolph S. Dennett	2	1	27	Center Conway Cemetery

I hereby certify that the above and foregoing is a true transcript of the records of all births marriages, and deaths that has been reported to me for the year ending December 31, 1938.

LESLIE C. HILL, Town Clerk.

Lightning Source UK Ltd.
Milton Keynes UK
UKHW020916220119
335965UK00013B/1772/P